Peace
BY
Piece

Cheryl Fuller

Lakeside Connections Publishing

Lakeside Connections Publishing

Paperback ISBN: 978-0-578-24470-9
Hardback ISBN: 978-0-578-24534-8

Cover Photo © 2021 www.gettyimages.com. All rights reserved - used with permission.
Edited by Sherry Hinman, The Write Angle, Ontario, Canada

PRINTED IN THE UNITED STATES OF AMERICA

This book is dedicated to:

My son, Ian Fuller, who brings love and joy to my life every minute of every day (well almost ☺). Being the mother to this beautiful human being brings purpose and meaning to my life beyond the words I have to describe the experience.

My late husband, Al Fuller. My only regret is that he died before I completed all of my therapy so we never had the experience of a marriage in my healthy emotional and physical state. My gratitude for him always loving me in spite of my issues lies deep in my heart. His presence in my life and exposure to the opportunity of a healthy, loving family changed my life in a profound way.

My therapist, Ed Zimmer. This book would not exist if it were not for your wisdom, guidance, compassion, humor, loyalty, intelligence, patience, flexibility and constant love and care. In fact, I would not exist or have the life I have now without you and all of your gifts. I literally owe you my life and "thank you" just doesn't cut it, but I have to trust that you know and understand beyond any words I put on this page.

My family and friends who have been present in my life in too many ways to name, but clearly are the pieces that complete the contents of my heart.

The countless people who helped me survive an experience that could easily have ended very differently including custodians, counselors, teachers, grocery store clerks, the friends and families who let me sleep in their homes and the many acts of kindness that came my way when I needed them to give me the courage to wake up and face the next day.

Table of Contents

Part II: . . .You Must Speak in the Light!

PART I:
WHAT YOU HEAR IN THE DARK . . .

"And once the storm is over, you won't remember how you made it through, how you managed to survive. You won't even be sure, in fact, whether the storm is really over. But one thing is certain. When you come out of the storm, you won't be the same person who walked in. That's what this storm's all about."

—Haruki Murakumi

Foreword

WHEN I HAVE shared my story of childhood physical, sexual, and emotional abuse, I am often asked, "How did you survive?" I always feel inadequate with my response. While the question itself implies an act of heroism, my response is simply, "I just did." Whether we refer to it as human nature or our own innate response, we all have within us a survival instinct. In my journey, I have met many survivors who "just did." As children, we may have been faced with completely unnatural situations, but we also possessed the adaptability skills to make enough sense of the situation to survive it. This book is primarily about a journey to discover who we are truly meant to be—for some of us, in spite of our childhood, and for others, because of it. It is a journey not only about surviving but also about going beyond surviving to truly living. It is about finding calm within chaos. It is also about the work of unlearning lessons that were instilled in our most vulnerable minds at a time when we did not know how to question what we were being taught. It is a journey of finding peace within ourselves so that we can then share in healthy, loving, and intimate connections with the people and the world around us.

While we may each know the horrific reality that some children do not survive abusive situations, for many of us, the survival instinct brought us through the most challenging of experiences. If during your childhood another person took advantage of your young mind or body, this book is for you. In some cases, it may have been one incident of sexual abuse with a known or unknown person. For others, it was years of being told you were not good enough, not smart enough, not pretty enough, or just plain "not enough." Some stories are from "well-intended" families who may have chosen not to "spare the rod" to help their children grow to be well-mannered adults. Over the years, I have come to understand that the number of people who have been physically, emotionally, or sexually abused is enormous. This book is not about looking for blame; it is about becoming who we are meant to be, regardless of the early experiences of our lives. Survival in childhood often was about "just doing it." The challenge as adults is in *un*doing it and learning to live rather than just survive. Unlike our experience as children, when survival happened from instinct, the challenge of healing as an adult is far more purposeful and requires a constant choice to continue the journey.

This journey is long, slow, painful, rewarding, necessary, frustrating, and unique for every individual. I have spent my own life trying to skip steps, cut corners, "think" my way into healthiness, get others to do it for me, resist the process, deny the issues, and otherwise avoid whatever pieces I could. I have had moments of such clarity I was sure the journey was close to an end and other moments where the world could not have become any lonelier, darker, or more confusing. Ironically, I have come to understand that even those moments were necessary parts of my healing process.

I feel a kindred spirit to anyone reading this who has been through childhood trauma. I do not need to know your name or see your face to understand your struggle. I have had the pleasure (and sadness) of meeting many faces and hearing the names of many people who share my experiences.

I wrote this book for two reasons. The first is that it serves as another step in my own healing journey. Reflecting on where I have been and where I am now will continue to bring me to a greater peace with myself. The second is my hope that this book will fall into the hands of even one person who is a survivor and that somehow my words will touch them in a way that will move them further in their own journey toward wholeness.

Because I have this strong sense of kindred spirit, I wish I could offer my writing as a "how to" book on the path to healthiness. I certainly have read my share of wonderful books, but no book gives us step-by-step directions on how to complete our own journey, this one included. Just as each of our experiences of pain and horror are unique to us as individuals, the path for recovery is equally unique. Our healing journeys are similar to completing a puzzle. I once saw a piece of artwork that was a beautifully painted heart, broken into many pieces that resembled a puzzle. That picture became the symbol of my healing process. I have been putting the pieces of my heart back together to find a wholeness I have never before experienced. Just like with a regular puzzle, I suspect the faint lines where the pieces come apart will always remain, but, held together with the right glue, the heart can function just like one that had never been broken—perhaps even better.

I do not have the answers as to how to put your puzzle pieces together. Every one of us has a unique heart, and thus the journey to rebuild your heart will be equally unique. You will gather your pieces from many different sources and, as many small miracles, they will appear in your life at the time and in the manner that will best allow them to fit together (though it may not seem that way at the time). Sharing my story with you may help a piece or two fit together. As much as I wish that it could help you complete the entire puzzle, I can confidently tell you now—that "ain't gonna happen." Perhaps, though, it will bring a few more pieces to the table or maybe shift a couple that weren't fitting together quite right.

This book may also be helpful to those who love someone who went through trauma as a child. While every person has their own set of issues, the experience of trauma has common and long-term aftereffects. For those people in our lives who care about us, understanding and responding to those aftereffects is also painful, confusing, and challenging. Perhaps, some of the information in this book will offer you clarity and assistance in understanding and supporting your loved one.

Because each person's journey is unique, I suggest you use this book, like all of your resources, to meet your own needs. The book is presented in two parts. The first part, "What You Hear in the Dark...," is my journal of events that happened in my life. It is not in chronological order. As an adult, I often experience my life as a long walk through a minefield—a trigger here, a memory there, and I have stepped on another proverbial "bomb"—and this first part covers those experiences as they have come up. The second part, "...You Must Speak in the Light," shares my experience of healing from the many injuries I sustained from the daily abuse that went on for many years.

Use this book in whatever way it might be most helpful to you. Read it quickly and move on. Read it slowly and digest every part. Read the chapters that relate to the most pressing pieces in your journey right now, or start at page 1 and go through to the end. However you find yourself using my story and the process of my journey, I hope it helps you move toward discovering the person you are meant to be.

Read it with a presence of self-care. If something I have written is disturbing or triggering, please use your best resources to help you understand what is happening for you and use it as a healing piece of your journey. It is my hope and dream for you that the words you need to hear, the thoughts you need to consider, the feelings you need to feel, and the ideas you need to learn will come into your life in any way possible. Perhaps, you'll find some of those in the pages that follow. I wish you healing as you move forward, knowing that you can do more than survive—you too can find peace and truly live!

CHAPTER 1

Church

I GREW UP in a small town in Maine, with my father, my mother, and my three siblings: my sister, Yvette, who was six years older; my brother Steve, three years older than me; and my brother Paul, three years younger than me. We were a Catholic family. My father made sure we practiced this religion faithfully in the early years of my childhood, but expectations for me to attend church began to fade as I approached the middle school years. Prior to that, we would be in church most Sundays. I liked the sense of community in the church; an opportunity to hide in public seemed preferable to the nightmare that was happening between the walls of my house.

In church, my father would insist that I sit several rows behind the family, telling me that he could not have one of his failures within his sight and think about God. He would explain to others, "She hates her brothers and doesn't want to sit with them." My father seemed to believe that God had chosen him to be one of his disciples. During many lessons, my father explained it was his job, as assigned by God, to fix me and turn me into someone they could both be proud of. And if he failed, God would not allow him entry into heaven. Many times, in a drunken state, my father would tearfully beg me to stop being a horrible daughter and learn my lessons so he could be at peace with God when he died.

To a six-year-old, trying to figure out how to "be better," "be good," "be smarter," "be prettier," "be tougher" during lessons that made me feel bad, stupid, ugly, and weak was impossible—it was as though someone had asked me to grow wings and fly away, which later became a fantasy I would create while in the deep recesses of the cold cellar. The weight of needing to do the impossible at the expense of my father's ultimate salvation added to the cloak of guilt I would wear for many years to come. Nonetheless, I thought of church as possibly being the place for me to learn exactly what God wanted me to become. So, in addition to the break from the walls of the cold cellar, I welcomed our Sunday trips for the chance they gave me for understanding.

At the conclusion of the service, the priest would stand at the back of the church, shaking hands and greeting people as they left. On most Sundays, my father would place himself to the right of the priest to shake as many hands and warmly greet as many folks as the priest greeted. The calculated relationships my father formed with others in town helped keep his secret world safe from questions and scrutiny. As a result, the priest, along with the chief of police, the other foremen at the mill, the principal of my school, and the neighborhood doctor could all be found on my father's list of close friends. Watching my father being so well liked and respected by so many in our town cemented the idea in a little girl's head that the problem was indeed with her and renewed the internal drive to fix the problem.

We walk into church on the afternoon of the Good Friday before my seventh birthday. My father enters first. Mom didn't come with us. Yvette is walking right behind my father and holding my little brother's hand as he tries to jump up the steps instead of climbing them. Steve is following behind them and taps my brother on the head as if to try and distract him further. I am in my usual place at the back. We are here to walk the Stations of the Cross, and I'm feeling excited that my father has allowed me to come along. As directed, I carefully stay at the back of the crowd and move from station to station. I watch as Yvette works to keep Steve and Paul from talking and fidgeting. I can't really understand everything the priest is saying, but I need to concentrate and try to memorize it—on the way here, Daddy said I need to pay attention and learn these stations, so that's what I'm trying to do. I can't hear or see very well from the back, but I'll get in trouble if I try to move closer. The old woman next to me has a necklace in her hands and I can't tell what she's saying, but she keeps talking about Mary, and it makes it even harder to hear what the priest is saying. I listen hard and look at the statues of Jesus as people hurt him and he falls down.

When we get into the truck to go home, my father asks all of us if we have any questions and no one says a word. "Cheri, tell me what the first station is," my father snaps.

I carefully answer, "They tell Jesus he is going to die."

My father angrily responds, "They condemn him!"

I feel so bad for not remembering that word, but surprisingly, he tells me that's close enough and to go on to the second station.

"He carries his cross," I respond.

"Keep going," he demands.

"He falls down," I say. I pause, waiting for approval, but then decide just to keep going while I can still remember. "He sees his mommy," I say for the fourth station. Still no response, so I move forward, but the tightness rises in my stomach as I am starting to forget what comes next. "Someone helps him with the cross and he falls down again," I quickly utter because I cannot remember which happened first.

"You left out getting his face wiped," my father shouts at me. "Just stop and shut up, you stupid bitch."

I sit silently on the floor of the truck, needlessly repeating the steps in my head, hoping to get them right before I'm asked again, but the damage has been done.

When we arrive home, my father tells my siblings to go to their rooms. My mom must already be in her bedroom because I don't see her anywhere.

"Get down to the cold cellar," my father shouts at me.

I run downstairs as quickly as possible and sit in the dark corner, waiting to see if my fate will simply be him locking the door or if there will be another lesson before the imprisonment. While I sit very still, trying to get the stations of the cross right in my head in hopes of gaining some salvation, I hear my father go up and down the basement stairs a couple of times. *Why isn't he coming and locking the door so I won't escape?*

"Get out here!" he shouts.

I jump up and go out into the basement, excitedly reporting, "Daddy, I've been thinking hard and I'm sure I can now tell you the steps of the cross!"

He looks at me with an odd smirk, and my body immediately freezes as I anticipate the danger that I know is ahead. I see boards lying in the shape of a cross on the floor in front of me, and I know these will be used for my lessons.

"Take all your clothes off except your socks," he demands.

I know I'm going to learn the lessons on the Stations of the Cross in a way that means I will never get them wrong again.

"I cannot believe I have such a stupid child for a daughter." He grabs my arm and throws me to the floor, startling me.

I put my hand out to break my fall and my finger jams between the boards and the floor. My body lands on the top of the cross and the edge of one of the boards pokes into my stomach. I'm trying to think about the stations and the lessons, but I'm just terrified as he continues to yell, "I will not have a stupid daughter living in this house. God will not have it and I will not have it!"

My brain races to remember. "Station 1: Jesus is told he has to die. Station 2: Jesus carries the cross. Station 3: Jesus falls down. Station 4: Jesus meets his mommy. Station 5: Jesus gets help carrying the cross. Station 6: Jesus falls again. No, that's not right. Station 1: Jesus is told he has to die. Station 2: Jesus carries—"

He grabs my right hand. A sharp pain shoots through my body

and I feel like my head is going to burst. I try to pull my hand to me, and it won't move. I blink away tears as I try to figure out what he just did to me. Then I notice the hammer in his hand, and I focus on the blood I see dripping from my palm. As he repeats the ritual with my other hand and then my feet, my body jolts every time he hits a nail. I look down and watch my socks turn dark red as they soak up the blood from my feet. My body begins to feel numb, and I drift off to sleep with my mind still trying to remember which station number was someone wiping the face of Jesus.

I open my eyes and I can't see anything in the complete blackness of the cold cellar. I have no clothes on, but something is wrapped around each of my hands. I carefully lift each one, checking to be sure it's no longer attached to the cross. I do the same thing with my feet. I can feel the weight of something, but my socks are gone and have been replaced with some type of bandage. I lie very still as I feel the rhythm of the throbbing in my hands and feet and slowly fall asleep again.

After I've gone several days of waking briefly and sleeping again, my father releases me to go back into the house, where I discover that Easter has come and gone and only a couple of days remain of spring break, before I return to school on Monday. My hands and feet still hurt, but they're getting better. My mom changes my bandages and the throbbing begins to subside. I am so relieved to be out of the dark and damp cold cellar. I'm especially excited tonight, as I curl up in my soft bed. As I lie here quietly, I listen to my own breathing and feel a deep sense of relief that I have survived another round of lessons. As I curl my arms around my pillow, something rubs against me. I lift my pillow and pick up my bloody socks, which are tied together in a tight knot. I know instantly that these socks are my father's way of making sure I will always remember my lessons about the Stations of the Cross.

Many years later, when I was in my fifties, I began experiencing tremendous pain in my left foot. After I visited the orthopedic surgeon and went through an MRI, the surgeon determined that apparently a piece of my cotton sock from that experience had lodged in my foot and, in response to a foreign object, my body had built a protective shield around the piece of lint and kept it encapsulated. Unfortunately, the capsule had shifted when I lost a bunch of weight and was now sitting on several nerves, causing pain and numbness in my toes. I needed surgery to have the capsule removed. Going to the hospital is always a challenging experience for me because of the number of surgeries and hospitalizations I have experienced. As I lay in the operating room waiting for my surgeon, I replayed the memories of the experience that had caused the original foot injury and thought about the bloody socks he had left under my pillow to help me remember. In the moment I was being put to sleep for my surgery, I wondered how my father could have thought I would ever be able to forget.

CHAPTER **2**

The Housewarming

UNTIL I WAS four years old, my family of six was cramped into a two-bedroom mobile home on the front lawn of my paternal grandparents' property. We were so excited to be moving into a new home. In this new mansion, my older sister and I would share one bedroom and my two brothers would have their own room. No longer would the four of us be piled into bunk beds and forced to share a tiny living space.

It is a few months before my fifth birthday, and I am standing on the front steps of our new house. I am overwhelmed with its size— our new home has two stories, with three bedrooms and a bath upstairs, and a kitchen, living room, and den on the first floor. We also have a large basement and a big yard. We are all so excited for this change that we can't wait to move in tomorrow.

"Let's go back to the trailer and get some stuff, and we'll come back here and sleep on the floor tonight," my father says.

I run into the trailer and grab my pillow and blanket. Should I take my favorite stuffed animal or my Candyland game to play with my brothers and sister tonight? I grab Teddy and run back to be the first one in the car, ready to go "camp out" in our new estate, leaving all our other worldly possessions behind, to follow the very next day. Our new house is only two miles away, but it seems like we're moving to a new country! I'm crushed between my brothers in the backseat of the car, but I don't care as I think about all the rooms to explore in our new home.

At three o'clock in the morning (moving day!), the furnace in our mobile home explodes. I stand on the front lawn of my grandmother's house, holding my brother's hand, watching firefighters move around among the burned stuff on the ground. It smells funny, and smoke is still coming up from the ground. I try to recognize our stuff, but nothing looks familiar. My mother is standing, holding my sister's hand. She's crying and my sister is rubbing her arm. My father stands between two firemen and I listen hard to hear what they're saying.

"If you'd been sleeping in this trailer when it caught fire, you'd all be dead right now!"

My father laughs at the fireman's comment and I look up at him to try and understood what's so funny.

My father painted a Shuffleboard game onto the cement floor of the basement, and he goes down there sometimes with a case of beer and his friends and they stay there for hours. Tonight, we're having an official housewarming, now that we've been in our house for about a month. I spend most of the evening on the front porch, saying hi to my dad's friends as they arrive for the party. Then, we're sent to bed early and I lie in my bed, listening to people's voices and lots of laughing as I drift off to sleep.

"Wake up, Cheri," my father says, shaking my shoulder. "Your cousin Kim is here, and she wants to play. Come with me."

Wow. I get to go play and my sister has to stay in bed. I'm so lucky! I love our new house.

We move very quietly to keep from waking the others as we don't want them to know our "special secret."

Daddy doesn't usually like me very much. He likes my brothers much more. He likes boys because he says they're strong and courageous, but girls are weak and needy. My sister is pretty strong, so he tolerates her, but I always do things that embarrass him and make him mad, so I know he doesn't really like me very much. But tonight, he picks me to wake up and bring down to his party.

As he takes me by the hand and leads me down the stairs to the first floor and then to the basement, I feel so special! But as we begin walking down the basement steps, my stomach begins to tighten, and I want to turn around and run back to my room. Something doesn't feel right. As I try to pull my hand away, my father grips it harder and pulls me with him down the stairs.

A few men stand around with beers and cigarettes in their hands. The room is smoky and smells yucky. Kim stands in the corner with no clothes on and she looks at me with a hard, blank stare.

"Take off your pajamas!" my father yells over the music. I look up at him and he looks mad. I know I have to follow his directions, but I don't want to take off my pajamas in front of all of these men. But I slowly step out of my pajamas and stare at the floor because I don't want to look at my father or any of these men.

"Get into the dog's crate," my father says to me and my cousin. I curl up and hug my knees. I peek over the tops of my knees and watch the men walk around, drinking and laughing. Sometimes, one of them comes close to the dog crate, stares at us for a minute, laughs, and then goes back to the group. One of the men walks over to us in the crate and pours his beer over our heads then laughs and turns back to the others. After a long time, my father comes over and reaches into the crate and grabs me. I push myself further back into the crate and start crying. This makes him madder and he tries to reach further to grab me.

"Get out here right now!" he shouts.

"Never mind, Max. This is supposed to be fun, so just leave her alone if she doesn't want to come out," one of the men shouts.

My father's brother steps forward. "My daughter will be happy to come out and join the party, won't you, honey?" he says to Kim.

Kim looks at me and says, "It's OK—I'll go."

For that moment, thanks to her, I'm spared. She gets out of the crate and they shout at her to dance to the music. I watch as my uncle touches all parts of her body, and I curl up into a tighter ball at the back of the dog crate.

After a short time, a woman comes down to the basement, calling for her husband. I watch her face become angry as she looks around the room.

"You should all be ashamed of yourselves for what you're doing," she shouts. "Fran, get up here. We're leaving."

Several of the men raise up their beer bottles and laugh as Fran says good night to the guys. Uncle Bobby tosses Kim her clothes and tells her to get dressed.

My father throws my pajamas into the crate. "Get dressed and get the hell to bed."

I put on my pajamas and slip past everyone running upstairs. My mom is in the kitchen, visiting with other women, and they all stop talking when they see me.

"Get to bed, Cheri," my mother says.

I run to my room, sneaking back into my bed, being careful not to wake my sister.

As I thought back on what my father later referred to as "one hell of a housewarming party," I was overwhelmed by a mix of complicated feelings. As I'd watched what happened to Kim and understood that it had happened to her because I would not come out of the crate, I began to absorb the layers of guilt that would become my survival garment for the rest of my childhood. Under the guilt, I could hide my fear, my pain, my anger—all of it could be consumed by guilt and I would merely need to learn how to keep breathing under the weight of the knowledge that my behaviors, and often just my very presence, brought harm to others.

As I thought about the reaction of the men when they were confronted by Fran's wife, the images of them laughing and raising their beer bottles lingered in my memory and I was keenly aware that they held no shame that night. In that twisted situation, it was the little girls who carried the burden of the shame for many years to come. I also learned that night that my reaction of hiding and crying in the back of the crate fueled my father's anger as though I had thrown kerosene onto a fire, and it would be many lessons later before I would learn how to control my natural reactions to unnatural circumstances.

CHAPTER **3**

The Cold Cellar

*You lock the door. You shut me in this cell. The darkness.
The silence. This is my hell.*

CLICK. A SIMPLE, momentary sound. It's just a click. So quick and
quiet one might not even notice. And yet, at five years old, my body
responds as though I am a trained Pavlov's dog. I become tense and
rigid. My brain immediately goes to work. *Am I hungry?* If I am al-
ready hungry, the panic will wash over me with intensity and sharp-
ness. If I am not, the panic will slowly roll in like the waves of a
changing ocean tide.

I have been locked into this room. In my house, it is referred to as
the cold cellar. In any other basement in Maine, it might be used to
store homemade bread and butter pickles, canned tomatoes, or the
green beans from last summer's garden. But in my house, while some
of those items are placed on shelves too high to reach, the primary
purpose of this room is to keep me locked up. Keep me in the dark-
ness. Keep me in the silence.

The room is small, maybe five feet by five feet, with a low ceil-
ing—too low to allow a grown man to stand comfortably. It's made
of dirt and dug into the side wall of the basement. The dampness im-
mediately sets off a shivering reflex in my body. It smells dank and
heavy, and sounds seem to disappear. When the door is closed and

I'm locked inside, I am in complete and total darkness. There are no windows and, once the outer basement light is turned off, there is not even a hint of light in the crack around the door. If I put my hand up in front of my face, I cannot see even its shadow. In this room, there are no shadows. In this room, at five years old, I learn to touch my eyeball to determine if my eyes are open. In this room, when the door is first closed, I have an orientation of where I am sitting on the cold, dirt floor. I fight to stay awake as long as possible because once I fall asleep and then open my eyes, I lose all my sense of orientation.

As the minutes become hours and the hours become days, I crawl along the floor to seek out the door as a point of reference for locating where I am in the room, but this ritual becomes dangerous. It is dangerous because I am now unaware of where in this dungeon I relieved myself and went to the bathroom. I can choose: know my location relative to the door or risk crawling through my own urine and feces.

The room is cold—a coldness that seems to be venting directly from the bones inside of me. Sometimes, I have my clothes to delay the cold or protect some pieces of my body, but at other times I am naked; he stripped my clothes from me before throwing me into the cold cellar, and now I'm aware that they lie in a pile only inches from me, but on the other side of the locked door, existing only as a picture in my mind. They tease my brain into imagining them helping me. So, I learn to negotiate with myself. If I sit on my right hand for a while it will feel warmer; then I can switch to my left. If I hold my big toe between my fingers it will retain some feeling and then I can switch to my pinky toe. I begin to take inventory of my body and develop rotating patterns of focus. I study all possible positions. Is it warmer to lie on the dirt floor curled up in a ball or to sit upright but pushed against a wall? My mind becomes convinced I can feel differences in my choices where none actually exist. My body, all of it, each and every cell, is cold.

The silence is excruciatingly loud. With nothing to see, I become superbly sensitive to any sound that might keep me connected to the world outside this room. Unable to decipher night from day, I detect every sound as a clue. Are those footsteps in the kitchen more than one person, perhaps indicating a gathering for a meal? If so, I need to pay attention to how much time passes before there is movement of people leaving the room, as breakfast will be shorter than lunch, lunch shorter than dinner. Is the water running for an extended time? This could mean that Mom is doing afternoon laundry, or someone is taking an early morning bath. Or, if the water is on for only a brief time, maybe it's just a lone toilet flush in the middle of the night. Or is there no sound at all—nothing but the sound of my own breath confirming I am indeed still alive? Has everyone left the house or just gone to bed for the night?

How long before I will hear a noise, any noise, because that will tell me for sure that I am still alive and connected to the world, even if I am locked away in here. I have to keep my mind busy until I hear a sound because if my brain is working then I must still be alive.

I can count. I know how to count to ten: 1 . . . 2 . . . 3 . . . 4 . . . 5 . . . 6 . . . 7 . . . 8 . . . 9 . . . 10.

Maybe I'll practice my alphabet because that will take longer: A . . . B . . . C . . . D . . . E . . . F . . . G . . . H . . .

After years of practice, I am very skilled at keeping my brain busy: Z . . . Y . . . X . . . W . . . V . . . U . . . T . . . S . . .

$8 + 6 = 14$. . . $10 - 4 = 6$. . . $9 \times 4 = 36$. . . $8 \times 2 = 16$. . .

I need to remember what I did to make Daddy mad, so when he asks me, I will have the right answers and he will let me out of here.

Do not speak until I tell you to. Do not speak until I tell you to. Do not speak until I tell you to.

I spoke when I wasn't supposed to. Do not speak until I tell you to. I won't do it again. I won't speak until I am told to. I remember the rule. Do not speak until I tell you to. I remember.

Decades later, I went back to my home on Third Street. I explained to the owner that this was the house I'd grown up in and I wondered if I might be able to take a look around. He invited me in and gave me a tour of the house. From my adult perspective, I laughed at my memories of this house as a mansion, when in reality it was a relatively small, two-bedroom home (the wall between my brother's room and my room had been removed to make it one large bedroom). As we finished the tour and I was preparing to leave, I asked if I could see the basement. He hesitated, looking curious, but he granted my request. We took the steps down into the basement and for a moment I wondered if I had done enough healing to be making this trek, but I really wanted to see the cold cellar again. As we walked down the stairs, I asked whether the "cold cellar" was still there.

He replied, "You mean the bunker? Yeah, it's there."

It was still there but in a slightly altered state. The door had been removed and a cement bench had been added inside the room that was currently stacked high with old magazines and newspapers. An overhead light had been added. I could not actually take myself over the threshold and enter the room. I felt relief that the door was gone and the room could no longer imprison a confused and frightened child. I liked that light had been added so that darkness could never again exist in the same way. That darkness haunted me for years. In my adult life, I would awaken from another torturous nightmare, and sometimes I would run to a closet and try to replicate the ironic feeling of safety of my dark prison, but it would never be as dark. The darkness of the cold cellar was different and almost impossible to imagine or replicate in a world where there is always light emitting from a cell phone charger, under the cracks of a door, or around the edges of window blinds. As I stood there looking at the cold cellar, my mind and body flooded with memories and I found it challenging to stay in the moment. I thought about all the lessons and the obsessive thinking I had engaged in to try to prevent my imprisonment from stretching from minutes to hours, from hours to days, from days to weeks. Every cell in my body suddenly wished the cold cellar could be blown up and destroyed. But even if that could happen, I knew it would still exist in the darkest, saddest corners of my mind.

CHAPTER 4

Lemons

VERY EARLY IN my childhood, I learned that to cry was the equivalent of committing some type of heinous act. In the natural world, a child relies on crying from the moment of birth, to communicate discomfort, pain, hunger, loneliness, and every other emotion. But in my world, crying was removed as an option for expressing any experience or emotion. Because crying is such a natural reaction, snuffing it from a child's experience requires many long hours of lessons.

The edge of a knife slowly slices along the palm of my hand. I feel the sharp pain instantly. The drops of blood well up until they pool and then spill between my fingers. My brain is fully aware of the experience and my eyes want to tear up, but for every tear that falls from my eye there will be another slice. I cannot stop the tears, and I feel the wetness on my cheek. Can I discreetly wipe it with my shoulder without him noticing? Of course not, because he is staring and watching intently for any sign of weakness. Another slice across the palm. Another tear escapes.

After a while, we have to switch to the other palm as it has become too challenging to see where to cut through the pool of blood. I am not sure how much time has passed, but if I concentrate on how much my legs hurt from standing here this long, perhaps I will not notice what it feels like as the knife cuts into me. I did it! A full slice across the center of my palm and not one tear escaped!! I look at my father with a sense of pride and a craving for any sign of approval. He nods and takes the knife over to his workbench. Both of my hands are burning, and I know I have a mess to clean up from the blood that has dripped onto the basement floor, but inside, the familiar, small sense of relief for having survived another lesson begins to grow. My father reaches into a paper bag on the bench. I cannot see what he has in his hand, but I see him pick up the knife again. I smell it before I see it—the pungent smell of a fresh-cut lemon. He walks toward me, barking orders to hold out my hands. He grabs one hand and begins to squeeze the lemon, spilling juice into each of the cuts. The sting seems to start at the very top of my head and bursts through every nerve in my body. Multiple tears fall from my eyes and the lessons begin again.

CHAPTER 5

The Animals

WE HAD MANY pets when I was growing up and I really loved every animal we had. I could connect with the pets even if it was from across the room, as I sat in my corner and they lay on their piece of the floor. I related to the pets because we were often treated in the same manner. Sitting on the furniture was against the rules for both of us, except I was fortunate to have a bed that I was permitted to sleep in most nights. At dinnertime, I often sat under the kitchen table with a dog or a cat, and my father would drop scraps of food on the floor. We would race to see who could get that tiny bite of food first. As a small, hungry child, the internal battle of wanting and needing the food for myself, while caring about whether my dog or cat was hungry, became the familiar script of choosing between my needs and someone else's that would haunt me for most of my life. In most families, a pet adds joy, love, companionship, and opportunities to grow responsibility. In my family, the animals often became objects used to teach me "lessons" about toughening up, blame, guilt, and ultimately the complicated ideas about attachment.

Big Boy

Big Boy was a beautiful, protective German shepherd who kept watch over me and my siblings for several years. In his desire to keep us safe, he bit the meter reader from the electric company—twice.

When someone would come to our house, Big Boy would race to the front door, jump up on his hind legs, and begin ferociously barking in a manner that would scare even the toughest of people. I admired Big Boy for his confidence in ruling the roost. My father did too. Unlike most of the pets we had that my father ignored, Big Boy often garnered the rare moments of positive affection that my father would ever exhibit toward anyone. As Big Boy lay on the floor next to my father, I would see my father occasionally reach down, pat his head, and mumble "good boy." I have an awareness now of how my expectations changed over time. At that point in time, I no longer fantasized about sitting on the comfortable sofa but lowered my expectations in hopes of garnering the attention Big Boy received. In these moments, I longed for my father to move me from the corner and let me sit next to him on the floor so that he might occasionally reach down and pat my head.

Everyone has gone to bed. I'm sitting in my corner in the den, hoping to be released to go upstairs. As an avid shooter, my father prefers to load his own bullets and shells. He is sitting in his corner, building his ammunition.

I'm getting very sleepy, but I need to stay awake so he doesn't send me to the cold cellar—I really want to sleep in my bed tonight. If I move my body that will help keep me awake, but I can't move too much because if I catch his attention it will make him mad and I will go to the cold cellar for sure. My bed is so much more comfortable than the cold cellar. I have to stay awake. I'm so scared and don't know whether to be still or move. I'll move my fingers for two seconds and then get still again. 1 . . . 2 . . . OK, I'll be still now until I count to thirty and then I'll move my toes. 1 . . . 2 . . . 3 . . . 4 . . . 5 . . . 6 . . . I see Big Boy sound asleep over there. I want to go to sleep too, but not here and not in the cold cellar. Big Boy is awake and moving. He's getting up and coming toward me. No, Big Boy! Don't come over here. I'm trying to tell you with my eyes to just stay there. I'm not going to look at you, Big Boy. Stay away! Daddy hasn't noticed him yet. I'm not sleepy anymore. I'm so scared. Please stop, Big Boy! I'm ignoring you. Just lay down. Not here. Not next to me. If I push you away, he is definitely going to see that. Your head feels so good on my lap. Just go to sleep and maybe he won't notice. Just be still. I'll show you how. I'm not supposed to touch you, but if I push your head out of my lap, he might see that. Let's just both be very still.

I feel the grip of his hand in my hair and the strain on my scalp as he yanks me from my sleeping state, pulling me across the floor, through the kitchen and out the front door into the cold and dark of the night. He drags me on my back, down the steps of the porch, and across the snow to the yard behind the garage.

Even though it's nighttime, it's not as dark out here as in the cold cellar, but it's so cold. I think the cold cellar is warmer than this. I wonder if he will just take me down to the cold cellar. I shouldn't have fallen asleep. My lesson will be about falling asleep. I'll tell him I know how to stay awake. I'll tell him I will practice in the cold cellar if he wants me to go there. I know I won't be in my bed tonight. He's taking me a long way behind the barn. I think I'm going to have to sleep out here tonight. I shouldn't have fallen asleep. I'm so mad at myself. I knew I wasn't supposed to go to sleep.

I understand. I know the rule not to fall asleep, but I did anyway. I know the rule not to touch the dog, but I did anyway. I understand why I have to sleep outside. I can do this. It's just so cold. Why hasn't Daddy said a word to me? He probably knows that I already know the rules and just forgot. He must be so disappointed and mad at me. He's leaving me here, behind the barn in the snow, but I understand. I remember my lessons—do not go to sleep until I tell you to. Do not touch the dog unless I tell you to. Do not go to sleep until I tell you to. Do not touch the dog unless I tell you to. I'll remember, Daddy. And when he comes back in the morning, I will be able to recite my lesson. I'm just going to crawl into the smallest, warmest ball and, if I say my rules a hundred times each, I bet it will be morning and I can go back in the house. Do not go to sleep until I tell you to. Do not touch the dog unless I tell you to. One. Do not go to sleep until I tell you to. Do not touch the dog unless I tell you to. Two."

What was that noise? There's Big Boy, running through the snow. He's peeing. I bet Daddy let him out to go to the bathroom. Here comes Daddy. Why does he have his shotgun with him? I think it's too dark for him to shoot his targets tonight.

"Big Boy. Come here."

Big Boy stopped his late-night rompings through the yard and came up to my father. My father instructed me to hold Big Boy's collar and told him to lie down. Big Boy did exactly as he was told. So did I.

"You seemed to like him sleeping in your lap," my father said.

"I remember the rules now, Daddy. Do not go to sleep until I tell you to and do not touch the dog unless I tell you to. See? I remember. I'm sorry I forgot, but I remember now!"

My father stood up, turned and walked two or three steps away from us and stopped. He turned back around, raised the shotgun and shot Big Boy four times.

"Don't cry. Don't cry. Do not go to sleep until I tell you to. Don't cry. Do not touch the dog unless I tell you to. Don't cry." The tears start rolling down my cheeks.

"You liked him sleeping with you, so now he can sleep all night with you," my father said as he turned and walked away.

Smokey

While I love all animals, I tend to enjoy dogs more than cats, though cats were numerous over the years of my childhood. Sadly, I believe they were easier for my father to access and to use as fodder for his lessons. Smokey was a dark gray, very large, and as typical, very independent cat. He did not seem to have any particular favorite people in the house and kept to himself most of the time. Nonetheless, he often provided entertainment for me by giving me something to watch when I sat alone in my corner.

My father built a homemade wood splitter that he kept in the side yard next to the garage and would use it to cut wood to stockpile for our Maine winter weather. It was my job to pick up the split pieces from the ground and carry them to the stack against the wall of the garage. It was hard work for a little girl, but I appreciated being outside and not having to sit still, so I approached the work with enthusiasm.

It's so warm and beautiful out here today. I don't even mind having to lug this wood. At least I'm not in the cold cellar or sitting without moving in the den. If I can just pick up the pieces quickly, he'll be happy with my work. There's one. Ouch! What was that?!

A second piece of wood falls on my head. Reflectively, my hand shoots up and I rub my head and wince with pain.

Don't show him it hurts. Quick, just go back to picking up the wood. Put a smile on your face and keep moving. Don't pay attention to the blood on your fingers. Just keep moving. Don't make any noises.

"You OK?" he shouts over the loud engine noise of the splitter.

I nod with an enthusiastic yes and quickly reach down to pick up another piece of wood, hoping to keep everything moving along. I can feel my eyes tearing up but don't cry. If I just keep my head down and pick up this wood, he won't see the tears in my eyes.

As if watching a movie in slow motion, I notice the drop of water as it leaves my face and falls to the back of my hand. I quickly glance up at Daddy, and I can tell he saw it too.

Oh no! What lesson will this be? I shouldn't have let that tear out of my eye. I shouldn't have let the piece of wood on my head hurt me. I should have been tougher. I'm so scared because I don't know what the lesson will be. Should I tell him I'm sorry or will that make him madder? Should I just keep working? I don't know what the best thing is to do.

My father turns off the wood splitter and I watch as he walks away and heads for the front steps of the porch. I notice Smokey, curled up in a ball and basking in the sun.

Run, Smokey. Run! I try to tell him in my head to run, but he doesn't hear me and barely moves as my father grabs his collar and pulls him into his arms.

A fire begins to burn in my stomach and I no longer feel the sting from the wound on my head that started this lesson.

Smokey is going to pay for me being weak and letting my eye cry when I got hurt. I should've been stronger. I feel like I'm going to be sick. I can't be sick. That will make it worse. Maybe it will just be a little hurt for Smokey. Maybe I can get him to hurt me instead of Smokey. If I say that, will it make him madder? I don't know what to do!

"Get up," he shouts at me.

I jump up. If I do everything quickly and just as he says, maybe it will just be a small lesson and only hurt a little.

He flips the switch and the loud noise of the splitter roars into life. Smokey startles and squirms in my father's arms as he tries to escape. My father calls me over to the splitter.

"Pick up that rope."

I have to carry out every order as quickly and smoothly as I can. I don't understand what is happening. Are we still cutting wood? What is he doing with Smokey? Why isn't there another log in the splitter? The splitter is so loud. It's scaring Smokey. He will settle down if we turn off the wood splitter. Should I suggest that? Should I turn it off? What am I supposed to do? Why is he tying Smokey to the shelf where the log goes? What is he doing? Is Smokey going to have to sleep there all day? Smokey, please stop fighting him. That makes him madder. Just be still. I'll show you how.

"Cheri, get on the other side and hold the cat's paws the way I am."

My father is holding one front paw and one back paw, so I do the same. My father lets go for a second and flips a switch. The wood splitter begins moving and I watch the blade getting closer to Smokey.

Smokey is going to die. We are going to kill Smokey right now.

I do not understand what is happening. I'm trying to let go but my hands won't move. My father is watching me and I can't move. I know your mouth is open, Smokey, and I think you're crying, but it seems like it's a long way away from me and all I can hear is the wood splitter. I can see blood spilling on my hands, but I can't feel it. My body doesn't seem to be connected to my head. I don't understand what is happening. I think my eyes are starting to make tears. I have to stop that. Tears are why Smokey is dying. I have to stop the tears. I have to be very still. I have to be very numb. 1 . . . 2 . . . 3 . . . 4 . . . 5 . . . 6 . . . Do not show pain. Do not cry. A . . . B . . . C . . . D . . . E . . . F . . . I'm so sorry, Smokey. I'm so very sorry. I love you. I'm sorry I showed it hurt when the log hit me in the head. I'm sorry I can't let go of your paws. $4 + 2 = 6$. $10 - 8 = 2$ . . . I'm sorry, Smokey. Do not cry.

As the splitter slices through Smokey's body, he quickly stops moving. As his body becomes still, I realize I have finally learned how not to cry.

Snowball

My father worked as a foreman in the local paper mill. My mother never worked outside the home. She was dependent on my father for everything. She never had a driver's license, so if she wanted to leave the home, my father was usually the one to take her anywhere. My mother was completely invested in everything being "OK"—especially my father. She spent a great deal of energy ensuring his needs were met and whatever he wanted was always what happened. She loved her children but was limited in her abilities to demonstrate that love or to ever challenge my father with his many rules and expectations. One of his rules was that you must never ask for anything. It may have taken me a year or so to learn this rule, but I did eventually. I learned that the consequences of asking my father for anything would be detrimental for me so I did not ask.

One evening, my father was taking my mother to the grocery store. His annoyance with her for asking him for anything was obvious, but it was usually less physically violent and more of a verbal rant.

My pet hamster was out of food and, knowing I could not ask my mother, with my father present, to get more food at the store, I carefully wrote a note and hid it in her coat pocket. As they were leaving, when my father's back was turned, I signaled to my mother to look in her pocket. She looked down and gave me a knowing nod, indicating she saw the paper.

When they got home from the store, I stayed seated on the floor in the corner, in my designated spot, and listened as my mother put away the groceries in the kitchen. I heard the front door open and close, so I knew my father had come in and out, though I was not certain enough that he was gone to try to speak to my mother. At one point, she walked through the den and I saw a bag of hamster food in her hand. She did not look at me or speak to me in the corner, but she walked the bag upstairs and came back through, empty-handed. I breathed a little lighter, knowing she'd seen the note and now my hamster would have food.

It's eight o'clock and I've been released from the corner to go to bed. I run upstairs, find the food under my pillow and feed my hamster a heaping pile of food. Knowing what it's like to be hungry, I feel a sense of pride in having secured food for Snowball without incident. I fall asleep a little faster and easier.

I feel someone grabbing my foot and open my eyes to see my father's furious face as he pulls me out of my bed and onto the floor. I try to get up but quickly fall on my back as he drags me into the hall and down the stairs to the first floor. As we come around the corner into the kitchen and head for the basement door, I see my hamster's cage under my father's other arm.

What's happening? I don't know what is going on. Why does he have Snowball's cage? Is he putting me in the cold cellar? What did I do wrong? Did I fall asleep too soon? No, he released me to go to bed. Did I forget to clean up something? What did I do?

He drags me down to the basement as I try to hold my head up, but it keeps banging against each step. It hurts, but I'm careful not to react or make a sound. My stomach is starting to burn. I'm getting really scared and I can't figure out what I did or what's going on. I can't let him see that I'm afraid or confused.

When we get to the basement, he drops my leg and I slowly sit up, being careful not to wince, as my back is really hurting.

"Get over here," he shouts from his workbench.

As I approach, I see a small slip of paper and realize it is the note I wrote to my mother.

"Cheri, you stupid idiot. You know the rules. You're not allowed to ask for anything. I'll tell you what you need and want," he shouts.

"It wasn't for me! It was for Snowball. He was out of food. I wasn't asking for anything for me!"

"Come closer," he says, and I watch as he takes Snowball out of his cage.

No, please don't hurt Snowball. Should I beg him not to hurt him or will that make it worse? Do I just stay quiet? He's going to hurt Snowball—I just know it. Will it make him madder if I tell him not to? Should I offer for him to hurt me instead? Should I repeat that I know the rule and explain that I thought it was OK because it wasn't for me? Or should I just stay very still and quiet? I'll ask him in my head to please not hurt Snowball, but on the outside, I'll stay very quiet.

My father reaches up for a saw mounted above the bench.

I quickly put my hand up on the table. "You can cut me," I offer. "That will teach me my lesson, I promise."

He looks down at me and laughs. "Too easy. You're the one who broke the rule. If Snowball is so important to you that you break the rules for him, then you will be the one who has to get rid of him."

The fire in my stomach blazes. In the next few minutes, I do exactly as I'm told and slowly torture Snowball by cutting off each of his legs. I don't understand what is happening. I see my hands on the saw and I'm telling them to stop, but they don't. I see Daddy watching me and I just keep cutting at Snowball. Go to sleep, Snowball.

Just be very still and quiet. I'm sorry, Snowball. I just wanted you to have some food. I didn't want you to be hungry, but I'm sorry I did it wrong.

I can't feel anything. The room seems like it is getting smaller. I'm almost done Snowball. I'm sorry. By the time I get to the fourth leg, Snowball is not moving anymore, and I find that place deep inside of me to hide my tears. My father picks up Snowball's body and throws it in the trashcan. He takes the four amputated legs and wraps them in the note I wrote to my mother. He hands me the paper.

"Go to bed and leave the note with the legs in it under your pillow until I tell you you can get rid of it."

I sleep with the legs under my pillow for the next few weeks as a reminder not to ask for anything for me or for anyone else.

The cold cellar was barren of light, warmth, and any type of stimulation. There are not enough adjectives to describe the nightmare of this black hole. I believe my father's intense hatred of me often came from my sensitive nature—so many of his lessons were designed to toughen my heart. He learned quickly that a direct line to my heart was through my love of animals.

One of his strategies that was most difficult for me to tolerate involved giving me a kitten, puppy, guinea pig, mouse, hamster, rabbit, bird, or other animal just as he was locking me in the cold cellar for a few days. In the absence of all other interaction, I would attach quickly and easily to any other life found in the abyss. After several days of having only this animal to cling to, he would rip it from my hands and I would have to watch as he killed it, or even worse, I would be forced to kill it myself. I lost track of the number of times this routine occurred over the years of my childhood. I no longer remember all the names of the pets. The intended lesson: do not love anyone or anything until you are good enough for love. Part two of the lesson: if you do love someone or something, very bad things will happen to them because of your presence in their life.

He wanted me not to care for these animals, but I could not stop it from happening. I continued to love any animal placed in my arms— EVERY single time. I did get more skilled at hiding evidence of my feelings, but somehow, I think he always knew and thus another animal had to die.

The guilt I have carried throughout my life for all of these animals has been one of the toughest parts of my healing. Ironically, it also has been my greatest strength because in spite of these evil and inhumane rituals, my father's actions never hardened my heart. It still opens for the love of any stray animal, any pet, any breathing life. My kind and loving heart, the part of me that drew such hatred from him, later became the very part of me that contained the first glimmers of what I could use to learn to love myself."

CHAPTER **6**

The Deer

IN TRUE MAINE fashion, my father was an outdoorsman who loved to hunt and fish. These passions he shared with my brothers. After one deer hunting session, he returned home with his friends and retreated to the garage, where they began drinking and bragging about their kill. As was usual, they hung the deer by its hind legs, cut open the stomach and began cleaning out the deer.

My father comes and gets me from the house. "Follow me," he barks, and I quickly step in line behind him. When we reach the garage, I notice a pool of blood circling under the deer and more blood dripping from the deer as they reach in and grab pieces, pulling them out and tossing them into a nearby bucket.

"Use this towel and start cleaning up this mess," my father orders.

When I put the towel on top of the puddle of blood it quickly soaks it up and I move the towel in circles to try to collect it all.

My father shouts, "Like this, you stupid girl," as he grabs the towel and rolls and twists it over the bucket, causing the blood to drip from the towel into the bucket. He throws the soaked towel back at me and it lands on my shoulder. My shirt now feels wet and sticky.

This is gross, but I need to just get busy cleaning. I can't let him see that I think it's gross. It smells gross, too. *Just concentrate.* I put the towel back down on the floor and begin moving it around again. After the towel seems like it isn't picking up any more blood, I drag it over to the bucket. I try to lift it above the bucket and squeeze the blood the way he showed me, but I can't lift the whole towel, so I have to just squeeze one section at a time. My father becomes angry when the part of the towel I am not holding falls into the bucket. He picks up the bucket and dumps it all onto the floor and I have to start over.

My stomach is feeling sick. This isn't the first time I have had to do something gross, but this time, my stomach is making me feel like I'm going to throw up. 1 . . . 2 . . . 3 . . . 4 . . . 5 . . . 6 . . . 7 . . . 8 . . . Just think about something else. A . . . B . . . C . . . D . . . Mary had a little lamb, her fleas were white as snow, and everywhere that Mary went, her lamb was sure to go. It feels like I am never going to get all this blood off the floor.

About an hour into the cleanup process, my urge to throw up is getting stronger. I know if I get sick, my father will be really mad because he will think that means I am not strong enough. He will have to teach me how to be stronger. I have to not throw up. I can't stop my body from responding, so I try to be as quiet as possible as I begin to throw up. If I do it behind the bucket, he might not see. I can be very quiet. Maybe he won't notice. He's talking to his friends so he may not see me. He notices. I see that look in his eyes when he glares at me. My sick stomach begins to tighten as I watch him looking at me.

He starts to laugh. "Well, guys, it's been a fun day, but it's time for you to get to hell out of here."

I continue to scrub the floor and focus on my work, and I see him saying goodbye to his friends out of the corner of my eye. A smoldering fire grows in my now-empty stomach, and I wonder what lessons are going to happen now.

The garage door closes. My father takes his stepladder and climbs up to secure the deer's front legs, so it is now hanging from the ceiling of the garage. It looks a little bit like the hammock in the back yard. I watch as Daddy climbs down and walks over to me, where I am still scrubbing and staring at the blood on the floor. I wonder if some of my own blood will soon be swirling in the pool. He grabs me by the hair.

"I will not have some weak bitch as my daughter!" he shouts. "You are an embarrassment to me, and I will not have that! Puking at the sight of blood!! Fuck no—that will not happen again!"

He begins ripping the clothes off my body and drops them into the pool of blood on the floor. I stare at my clothes, amazed at how quickly they soak up the blood, when he grabs me by my hair and carries me up the ladder. He grabs my dangling arm and throws me into the stomach of the deer.

"Maybe if you spend the night here, your stomach will toughen up."

I panic as he climbs down. I want to beg him not to leave me. I want to get out of this sticky stomach, but I know if I beg him it will make him madder. He turns off the light and I hear the door close behind him. I'm all alone in the dark and I'm afraid to move.

As I lie here in the belly of the deer in the dark, I feel the stickiness of the blood. I carefully roll onto my side. I feel like if I move too much the deer might fall and we will crash to the floor. I begin trying to control my body's responses and thinking through my lesson so that I can toughen up my stomach. I try not to be bothered by the horrible smell. Everything I touch is so sticky. My fingers are stuck to each other and it's hard to pull them apart. The blood and other stuff is gooey and it feels like I dipped my hands in glue, but it smells much worse. I concentrate very hard and focus. But I can feel my stomach tighten and as hard as I try not to, I throw up again. My father is not here to see it, but I still feel scared and guilty that it happened again. After a few minutes I throw up again. I wonder if he will be able to see that I threw up. I begin very carefully trying to mix my throw-up into the blood so if he looks, he won't be able to tell. I need to hide the evidence that my stomach is still weak. As I continue to mix the blood and the throw-up, I notice the smell is not bothering me as much, and my sticky fingers are doing a good job of mixing the blood and throw-up and I'm not throwing up any more. Maybe my stomach is getting stronger. Maybe I have learned my lesson. I slowly drift off to sleep.

I hear the garage door open and when I open my eyes, I realize it must be morning. I lie very still and listen for what will happen next.

In a lighthearted spirit, my father shouts up to me, "Good morning, Cheri. Time to get up!"

I slowly and carefully peek over the side and look down at my father. He is smiling up at me and the look on his face is very pleasant. He doesn't look at me that way very often, but I guess he's not mad at me anymore. My stomach begins to relax. I feel relieved because I have survived. Another lesson completed and I have survived.

My father puts his arms up in the air, smiles at me, and says, "Come down from that messy thing."

I pull my gross and disgusting body from the belly of the deer and jump into my father's arms. Just as I leave the deer's stomach, my father steps back and I fall onto the cement floor. I scream in pain as I hit the floor. A sharp pain shoots through my left arm and I pull it close to my body. Something is very wrong with my arm and I look up at my father to see that he is laughing.

"It's going to be even harder finishing your cleanup with only one arm. You better get busy."

CHAPTER 7

Morning Routine

MY FATHER WAS a foreman at the local paper mill. In this small town, that was a position of prestige. He worked in a rotation of three shifts: 8:00 a.m. to 4:00 p.m., 4:00 p.m. to midnight, and midnight to 8:00 a.m. I don't remember exactly how it worked, but I think he worked five or six days and then had two or three days off and then would start the next shift in the rotation. For a young child, keeping track of such a fluid schedule presented a unique challenge. However, the consequences of not knowing exactly where he was and when he would be home were severe enough to force an obsession with managing the schedule.

There were different rules and routines, depending on the rotation. When he worked the day shift, I became a part of his morning ritual. When he left his bedroom to go into the bathroom, he would shout my name and I had exactly ten seconds to wake from my sleep, jump out of bed, and run down the hall to be in the bathroom with him before the door closed. If I arrived at the bathroom door and he was already inside with the door closed, I needed to run down to the basement and put myself into the cold cellar. He would be down before he left for work to close the door and I would remain there until . . .

This morning, I am able to wake up and run to the bathroom in less than ten seconds. He pulls me into the room, and I sit on the floor in this very small bathroom to watch his morning routine. He stands at the toilet and pees. Before he's done, he turns and finishes peeing on my head. He turns to the sink and begins brushing his teeth. As he finishes, he turns back toward me and spits his toothpaste onto my head.

As I sit on the floor, I notice how much better the toothpaste smells on me than his pee, but it stings when it runs into my eye. He reaches down and grabs my nightgown and pulls it off over my head. I don't like not having any clothes on, but I try not to let that show because I'm afraid it would make him mad. He grabs my arm and lifts me to the sink and tells me to sit on the edge. He squirts some foam out of a can and puts it all over his face. I wonder if he's going to put it on my face too. He reaches into the cabinet and takes out his razor. He grabs my hand and uses the razor to cut the end of my finger. I try to pull my hand back and he holds my finger tighter. I look at him hoping he will see something in my eyes that will stop him, but he just smiles and keeps cutting.

"Write the word *bad* on the mirror," he directs.

I slowly draw my finger along the mirror, leaving a trail of blood in the shape of the letters. I write the b and the a, but I don't have enough blood to make the d. I go back to the b and try to get some more blood on my finger. My father grabs my hand and makes another cut. More blood drips from my finger and I quickly go back to writing so I can use all the new blood I have. I am happy today's word is short and I only have to write three letters. I didn't like it last time, when the word was *stupid* and I had to have enough blood for six letters. And I'm happy I know how to spell *bad* because he got really mad at me when I didn't know how to spell *ugly* or *bitch*.

"Now look at that word. BAD. That's what you are, so just look at it and don't stop looking at it until I tell you to stop!"

I hope today is short just like the word. I hope I won't have to look at it very long today. I sit and stare at the word in the mirror.

Sometimes my eyes shift to my naked body, but I quickly look back at the word. I want to look in the mirror at what he is doing, but his eyes might see my eyes not looking at the word and I would have to have a lesson. So, I just keep looking at the word. The blood begins to dry, and I feel happy that I'm remembering to just keep looking at the word.

"What are you, Cheri?" he asks.

"Bad."

"Spell it!"

"B . . . A . . . D."

"OK. Now clean up your mess."

He turns on the water and I get my hand wet. My finger stings when the hot water hits it, but I tell my body not to flinch. I begin wiping the blood off the mirror. BAD. B . . . A . . . D. I know I will need to say it and spell it again after I have erased it, so I'd better practice. BAD. B . . . A . . . D. My father turns the cold water on in the tub. After he sees the word is gone, he picks me up from the sink and puts me into the cold water in the tub.

"Be sure to wash your hair. It stinks," he says as he turns and walks out of the bathroom. As I get my hair wet and begin to wash away the pee and the toothpaste, I feel really grateful. This was a good lesson. The word was short and easy to spell. I didn't have to stay on the side of the sink all day. I feel happy and try to ignore the stinging in my fingers as the shampoo seeps into the cuts.

CHAPTER **8**

School

I LOVED SCHOOL—THE opportunity to be around others, to sit at a desk, to eat in the cafeteria—I welcomed every second of the experience. So much so that, as an adult, I have spent my entire life working in schools, as a teacher, counselor, and school principal. I feel quite confident and extremely relieved to know that a situation such as mine would be much more difficult to hide today, because reporting procedures, identification skills, and general knowledge around child abuse increase our opportunity to uncover hidden secrets.

Without revealing my own history, I have used my experience to help find those children who come to school hurting and scared from the experiences happening to them at home. Interestingly, one of my greatest challenges is in helping others realize that the signs are not always the typical red flags—behavior problems, bruises, academic struggles, anger outbursts, excessive crying, and so on. While these certainly are cause to question what might be happening for a child, if I reflect on my own experience, I would not have fit into any of those descriptors. In fact, I was quite the opposite. I was the quietest student in the class. I was the perfect student, working hard for straight A's and teacher approval. I never cried or showed anger. My bruises were covered up or I was kept locked in the cold cellar until the evidence faded. Helping people notice the child who may be a little too quiet and a little too well behaved has become part of my mission.

My father did not like my feeling good about school. He did not like my feeling good about anything. If I happened to mistakenly show a strong feeling of like or desire for someone or something, it would become his challenge to get rid of the object of desire or change my feelings in some way.

School was no exception. He began showing up at school at recess time. I would see his truck parked across the street as he monitored my every move. I knew the rule: do not play with the other children. Do not play. Find a place and sit quietly until recess was over. I liked it when I could sit on one end of the bench and the teacher was sitting on the other end. I had to fight the cravings to slide down the bench and be next to the teacher, just to feel her presence close to me, but I never knew for sure when he would show up. So, I just imagined sitting close to her while safely keeping my distance.

As I got older, I would strategically place myself on the ground, in clear view of the window to the teacher's lounge, where I thought my teacher would be during her break. It is challenging to describe the dichotomy of desperately wanting to be seen while needing and hoping to remain unnoticed.

In fifth grade, I had a wonderful teacher, Mrs. Dodge. She was tall and thin, and her long, straight blond hair made me think she was the most beautiful person I had ever seen. My head full of curly hair became one of the traits my father abhorred the most about me. Probably because, if I went anywhere in public, many people would comment on the "beautiful curly hair your little girl has." This became a source of great anger for him and dragging me by those curls seemed the only relief for his feelings. I envied Mrs. Dodge her long, beautiful and very straight hair. Inside, she became a favorite person of mine, and I worked hard to be sure she would notice me sitting off by myself at recess time. As they say, be very careful what you wish for. She did notice. However, she did not approach me about it. Instead, she called my house. I learned early in my schooling that calling home would have severe consequences, so around second grade I started doing things that would minimize calls to my parents by making up notes to change the number in the school record, lying about my parents being at home, and so on. On this occasion, despite my actions, Mrs. Dodge had figured out how to reach my house. She did not mention to me that she had called home.

Sitting here under the table, I know dinner is pretty much over, as my siblings have already left the table. I didn't get much food tonight and I'm still hungry, but I would rather get away before my father has another beer.

"You can come out from under the table, Cheri," my father says.

"King, may I be dismissed now to go to my corner?" I quietly ask, remembering every word exactly.

"No, you may not, little shithead. We have something to talk about," he barks.

He sends my mother out of the room and reaches down and grabs my curly hair, pulling me out from under the table. My mostly empty stomach immediately begins to churn, and I'm scared for what is going to happen next. What have I done? What did I say? How did I move wrong? What rule have I broken? Was this a night I was not supposed to eat? I don't know what I did, and this isn't making sense to me yet. He grabs my arm and I try to stand up, but he's moving too fast and he drags my body along the kitchen floor. As we approach the cellar stairs, I try to prepare for how much it's going to hurt as my body bounces off each of the steps, but there is nothing I can do. I'll count the steps as we go. That will help. 1 . . . 2 . . . 3 . . . 4 . . . 5 . . . 6 . . . 7 . . . 8 . . . 9 . . . 10 . . . 11 . . . 12.

"Your mother got a phone call from your teacher today," he begins. "Your teacher seems to be concerned that you are sad and depressed. She says you don't ever smile at school. Is that true, Cheri? Are you not smiling at school?" he demands.

Smiling. Did I smile in school? Am I supposed to smile in school?

Is there a rule about smiling? I can't remember. Before any words have time to come out of my mouth, my father slaps me in the face. He grabs my chin and squeezes hard. My jaw tightens.

"Smile, dammit. Let me see you smile."

I try to smile, but he's holding my mouth so hard I can't really move my lips to make a smile. With his other fist, he punches me in the mouth. I feel the blood in my mouth. I try to pull away, but his grip is too strong. He grabs me by the arm and drags me over to his workbench, where he picks up a board.

"I can't believe I got a fucking phone call because you aren't happy! I'm the fucking one that isn't happy. Nobody worries about how miserable I am getting, stuck with you for a daughter. What about that? Do you think I'm smiling when I know I'm stuck with you every fucking day for the rest of my life? You will smile at school, goddamn it!"

My mind is listening and watching, and my body is being beaten, tossed, knocked to the floor, kicked and punched. Intense pain flares in my back, then my leg. He's hitting me with his belt, and it burns as it streaks across my back.

"Smile, dammit! Show me your teeth you're smiling so hard," he screams.

I can't feel my mouth anymore. I can still taste blood and I see at least one tooth fly across the floor. The punches continue, and I eventually can't see my father's anger anymore. I can't feel my body. I can't hear the shouting.

Over the next few weeks, I lie on the cold cellar floor as my body takes on the challenge of healing with limited food and water; no warm clothing; no bandages, ointments, or braces. I practice smiling as often as I can. At first, my mouth is too sore, but after some time I can make my lips curve up into a smile. I practice telling my mouth to smile while telling my eyes not to cry.

Almost a month later, my father takes me to school. We round the corner to my classroom, and I spot Mrs. Dodge. She smiles at me and I smile back with the biggest smile I can make. I walk to my desk and smile at every child I pass. Out of the corner of my eye, I watch for my father to leave. From my seat, I can hear him talking to Mrs. Dodge.

"Thank you for calling and for your concern about Cheri. Because of your call, we took her to stay with her aunt for a while and while she was there, she went to see a psychiatrist. It seemed to really help. She seems much happier now and I think you will notice she is smiling so much more. Thanks so much for your call so we could fix this problem." As he turns to walk away, he shouts to me, "You have a great day, Cheri, and I look forward to hearing how much fun you had when you get home tonight."

I nod and smile a great big smile.

CHAPTER 9

Bean Hole Beans

MY FAMILY OWNED a small, one-room camp, on a lake about thirty minutes from our house. Each summer, my father would host an annual event known as his big "bean hole bean" cookout. He had a large hole in the ground outside the camp. A couple of days before the cookout, he would build a fire in this pit and keep the fire going night and day until he had built up a bed of coals several feet deep. He would then prepare his beans in a big steel pot, seal the pot, place it into the coals in the pit, cover the hole with dirt, and leave the beans in the ground to cook for at least twenty-four hours. He would then invite all of his friends over and, at the appropriate time, he would dig out his treasure and share his bean hole beans with everyone.

Because this annual event happened during the summer, while I was back at our house in the cold cellar staying busy surviving, I was not a participant in the cookout. In the summer I was nine years old, however, my father's boss was going to be coming, and this year he asked to bring his kids. Because of his boss's expectation that the children would be paired up with their natural peers from our family, I had the rare experience of being included in the event.

I walk out the front door and down the steps of the front porch and look up, because the sun feels so good I just want all of my face to feel the warmth. I follow my father's directions to get in the car and I sit in my place on the floor in the backseat. My sister and brother Steve are sitting in the seat, and I'm trying not to move too much, or Steve will kick me to make more room for his legs. My mother and my younger brother Paul stayed at the house. I'm wondering where we are going, and I feel curious and excited but also worried that maybe I'm being included because it's someplace bad. After a few minutes of riding in silence, Steve asks our father where we are headed.

"If I wanted you to know where we're going, I would have told you."

After that, nobody talks, and I feel more worried than excited. After another fifteen minutes go by, I see my sister mouth the word "camp" to my brother and then I know we're on the road to camp. When we arrive, my father gives us jobs to do. He explains that people will be coming over to eat his beans, and we have a lot to do to get ready. I listen carefully and make sure I do every job I'm given as well as I possibly can.

Sometime later in the day, my father yells, "Cheri, get over here." I run to him, thinking about the last job I did and what I might have done wrong.

"People are going to be arriving soon," he tells me.

"Where do you want me to hide?" I ask.

"Fran is bringing his kid with him today, and you're going to play with her. Just do whatever she wants to do and keep her happy. I don't want any problems out of you today or there will be hell to pay. Do you think you can manage to stay out of the way?"

"Yes, Daddy. I'll let her do whatever she wants, and I'll make sure she has fun and you won't hear from me at all."

I find a tree and go and sit up against it, watching people come to my dad's party. He seems very happy to have everyone there and I see him as he pats everyone on their back or shakes their hand. I notice he has a beer in his hand wherever he goes, and I watch carefully to see if he calls me over to run and get him another one when he needs it. He hands a beer to every person as they arrive. I watch everyone pull in and I'm very curious about the girl that I have permission to play with. I see one man get out, and he opens the back door of his car, and out steps a beautiful girl with long red hair. I think she is a good girl because she was sitting on the seat of her car and not on the floor, so I know she's special. My father walks toward the man and hands him a beer. My father looks down at the girl and pats her head and smiles at her. My dad likes her. I can tell. After a minute, he turns and looks toward me with a nod, and I jump up and run over to them.

"Laura, this is Cheri, and she's going to play with you today and you are going to have a lot of fun. Isn't that right, Cheri?"

I nod my head and look at Laura. She is so beautiful, and I can see my dad likes her and I feel sad that I don't look like her.

"What do you want to do, Laura?" I ask.

"Let's go in the water!" she says and starts running down the hill to the lake, shedding her clothes, leaving her in her bathing suit. I love to swim, but I'm not supposed to go in the lake, and I feel confused about the rule of not going in the lake and my father's instructions to do whatever Laura wants. I look up at my father and he nods and lets me know I'm supposed to follow her.

Laura is already in the water when I get there, and I follow her in. I look back at my father to be sure it's OK for me to be doing this, and he is back to talking with his friends. Slowly, I swim out to Laura.

"I wish we had a lake to swim in. You're so lucky!" she says to me.

I smile and say "Yes, I am." But I don't feel lucky. I want to tell her that I usually can't use the lake because I'm in the cold cellar at my house, but I remember the rule about never talking to anyone about the cold cellar. I think about Laura being lucky because when she rides in the car, she sits on the seat and her daddy looks at her and smiles. I think she is really lucky, and I wish I could be Laura.

After we swim for a while, Laura asks, "What should we do now?"

"We can do whatever would make you happy," I respond.

"I'm hungry. Can we go get some food?"

My stomach feels hungry too, but for sure I know the rule about not asking for food. I don't know what to do. I'm not supposed to ask for food, but Laura wants food to be happy and I'm supposed to be sure Laura is happy. I keep looking at Laura and I try to get my brain to know what I should do.

"What's wrong with you?" she asks.

"Nothing. I'm fine. I'm just not sure what we have for food."

"Well, let's go ask," she says as she starts running up the hill. She runs up to her father and grabs his hand. "Daddy, I'm hungry. What is there to eat?"

My father is talking with someone else not very far away, and I am staying back and listening to Laura talk to her father. My father looks at me and I can tell he is not happy. He quickly looks at Laura's dad and walks over to Laura and pats her head.

"Well, Laura, if you're hungry, then certainly Cheri will get you something to eat, right, Cheri?" he asks looking over at me.

I nod yes, but my brain is wondering how to get her food without breaking the rules about opening the refrigerator or getting in the cupboards. I am not moving yet because I need to think about what to do. Then I remember the table we put up for food.

"Come with me, Laura!" I say as I move to the front of the house where the food table is set up. I hand Laura a plate and tell her to get whatever she wants. I feel really proud that I can make Laura happy and I didn't have to open the fridge or the cupboards, so I have not broken any rules. There is a lot of food on the table. I see sandwiches and potato chips and pickles and something in a big bowl that might be potato salad. I look back at my father and he is looking at me. I am hungry, but maybe not that hungry. I think it might be better for me not to take any food right now because Daddy didn't say I could eat. He just said I would get Laura something. But I am pretty hungry. I look back and my father is still watching me, so I just watch as Laura puts more chips on her plate and grabs a sandwich.

"Aren't you going to eat?" she asks.

"I don't think I will right now," I reply. "Maybe later."

"Ah, come on. I don't want to eat by myself. Here, have a sandwich," she says as she grabs another sandwich and hands it to me. If I don't take the sandwich, Laura will be unhappy. If I do take the sandwich and my father doesn't want me to, I'm going to be in trouble. My brain doesn't know what to do. I look back at my dad and see that he has turned and started talking to some other people. I take the sandwich and tell Laura we should go to The Rock to eat.

The Rock is a really big rock, just down the dirt road that leads to the camp. I've seen my big brother climb up The Rock with his friends. I've watched my little brother try to climb it, but he's too small. I've never been allowed to touch The Rock or try to climb it. But I know that if we eat our lunch at The Rock, my father will not be able to see us, and I can eat the sandwich Laura just handed me without my father knowing. I run ahead and get to The Rock before Laura. The sandwich tastes so good. Laura keeps talking, but I just keep eating. I wish she would give me some of the chips on her plate, but I know better than to ask, so I just watch as she eats them. I hear my brother's voice and look up to see him and another boy running down the road to The Rock. I don't want Steve to see me eating my sandwich because he might ask if Dad said it was OK for me to have it, or he might tell Dad, so I will just hold it behind my back. The boys walk up and tell us to move over so they can climb up The Rock. Laura gets up and starts to walk away, and my brother looks at her plate.

"Hey, can I have some of those chips?" he asks.

"Sure, I'm done. You can have the rest." She hands him the plate, and he shoves the chips into his mouth. He tosses the empty paper plate at me and tells me to be sure to put it in the garbage. My brother and his friend climb up The Rock, and Laura looks at me and says, "Let's climb up too."

I step back and look at her. I know I'm supposed to do what Laura wants, but I'm not allowed to climb The Rock. I don't say anything and just keep thinking about what I should do, when my brother reaches down and tells Laura to grab his hand. He pulls her up and she climbs to the top of The Rock and sits with the boys. I look up and see my brother looking the other way, so I put the last bite of my sandwich in my mouth. I stand there and hold the paper plate so I can put it in the garbage. I'm not going to try to climb The Rock. My brother may tell Daddy. I might fall and then Daddy would know. It's best if I just stand here and be quiet and let them have fun and forget about me right now.

After a while, they all jump down from The Rock and my brother shouts, "The first one to the end of the road wins!"

Laura looks at me and shouts, "Come on, let's go!"

I watch as they all begin running down the road. I'm not supposed to run. I'm not supposed to go to the end of the road. I am supposed to do what Laura wants. I slowly start walking. I wonder, if I walk slowly, will they get to the end of the road and come back before I go too far. 1 . . . 2 . . . 3 . . . 4 . . . 5 . . . 6 . . . 7 . . . 8 . . . I look back to see if my father is coming. I don't see him. I just slowly keep walking until I hear their laughing, and I know they're coming back. The boys run past me and Laura stops when she gets to me.

"Why didn't you come? Don't you like running? You have so much to do here. You have swimming and climbing rocks and roads to run with no cars. You're so lucky. I wish I could live here. But my house is nice too. You should come to my house and play! I'll ask my Dad if you can come play at my house someday."

I feel happy that Laura is happy. I want to tell Laura about the cold cellar. I want to tell her that I can't climb rocks and run on roads with no cars. I want to tell her that I want to go to her house to play, but for sure I know that is not allowed. I don't want Laura to ask her Dad because then her Dad will ask my father and my father will get mad.

"I don't want to go to your house to play. You probably have a nice house, but I don't think I would like to go there to play," I say in a quiet voice. I look at Laura and her face looks sad or mad or both.

She turns and runs back to the camp. I go after her and call her name, but she doesn't stop. When she gets back to the camp she goes up to her Dad and takes his hand.

I slowly walk up to her. "Do you want to come play, Laura?"

She shakes her head no. Her father reaches down and runs his hand along her long hair. She has beautiful hair. Not curly like mine.

"Are you ready to go, honey?" he asks her.

She nods her head yes. Her father and my father say their good-byes. Laura gets into the backseat of her car and sits on the seat. I wave at her, but she looks the other way. I don't think Laura is happy.

I decide to go sit quietly under the tree until my father tells me what he wants me to do next. I watch my father as he talks with his friends. He still has a beer and gives out more beers to his friends. The sun feels warm and I keep moving around the tree to keep the sun on my face. "Let's go, Cheri!" my father shouts. I jump up and run to the car. I crawl into the backseat and sit on the floor next to my sister's legs. I think about what a special day it has been. I got to go swimming. I had a whole sandwich for lunch. I touched The Rock. I walked partway down the camp road. I played with a friend.

As we enter the house, my father says, "Cheri, cold cellar," and I turn to the left and walk down the basement stairs to the cold cellar. As I lie down on the cold, damp floor of the cold cellar, I think about how warm the sun was on my face and I fall asleep.

I wake up and think about my play day. I am hungry! But there isn't any food here. I have to stop thinking about food. 1 . . . 2 . . . 3 . . . 4 . . . I think it must be nighttime now. I don't hear any noises. I bet everyone is asleep. A . . . B . . . C . . . D . . . E . . . F . . . I fall asleep and wake up several more times. I feel very, very hungry. I hear it! The door opens and someone is walking down the steps. I sit up and brush the dirt off. I wipe my face to be sure it is clean. The door opens. Ouch! The light instantly makes my eyeballs hurt, but I don't say ouch out loud. I remind myself not to hide my eyes. Just keep them open and they will stop hurting after a while.

"You can come out," my father says. Was his voice mad?

The next few days are a normal routine, but my father seems more mad at me than usual. He snaps orders at me. He keeps me in my corner or the cold cellar almost all the time. One evening, as I sit in my corner in the den, I hear him talking to my mother.

"Fran said Laura didn't have fun at the party. Laura said Cheri didn't want to do anything. She had to play with Steve and his friend. I gave Cheri one job to do and she couldn't even do it. All she had to fucking do was play with the little girl and she failed at that! I hate that kid."

I can't hear what my mother says back to him, but now I understood why he's so mad.

I hear about Laura's report over the next few nights. The more beer my father drinks, the more he yells at me about how much I failed. I know there will be a lesson, but what is it going to be and when is it going to happen? I try to just stay out of his way, but I know there will be a lesson, and my stomach feels sick waiting for it to happen. Every time my father speaks, I jump. I watch him even more carefully than normal because I know there will be a lesson.

Six days after the party, my father comes over to where I am lying in my corner in the den. He grabs my arm and lifts me off the floor. It's hurting how hard his fingers are grabbing me, but I have to be sure not to act like it hurts. As he drags me through the kitchen, my eyes lock with my mother's eyes for a split second as she looks up from the dishes she's washing. She quickly looks away and hollers for my brother to turn down the television.

My father opens the back door of the car and throws me onto the floorboard. This is going to be a lesson, but what is he going to do? I have to be strong. I have to not cry. I decide to pinch my arms and practice not crying. I have to think of a song I can sing in my head during the lesson. Happy Birthday is too short. I can't think of a song. I'll practice my multiplication facts. I can't see where we're going. It's too dark. I wonder how long before we are there. 1 . . . 2 . . . 3 . . . 4 . . . This road is bumpy. I think this might be the camp road. We're going to camp. I'm ready. 3 x 5 = 15. 4 x 6 = 24. Pinch and hold—1 . . . 2 . . . 3 . . . 4 . . . I'm ready for my lesson.

The car has stopped. He opens the door and tells me to get out. It's very dark and very quiet. There are no lights at our camp or at my grandmother's camp next door. We're all alone.

"Follow me, you little bitch," my father shouts.

I follow as close behind him as I can. 7 x 7 = 48. No, wait—49. I'm so stupid. I have to get this right. 7 x 7 = 49. Why are we going around to the front and not in the door? What is that light? His fire pit is glowing. He must be making more beans. Is there going to be another party? Is my lesson to practice playing with Laura? But it's dark and no one is here. There is no party. I look up at my father and his eyes look so angry. He looks at the pit and then at me. I can feel my belly getting very hot. What is he going to do? Is he going to put me in the pit and cover me with dirt like the beans? Am I going to die in the pit tonight? Where is the car? Should I run? No, he will catch me, and he will be more mad.

"I'm sorry, Daddy! I'm sorry I didn't make Laura happy. I promise I will play better next time. I'm so sorry, Daddy!"

He reaches down and grabs me around my waist. I think I'm going to throw up. No, don't throw up. That will be worse. What was I going to do during my lesson? Happy Birthday to you. Happy Birthday. No that wasn't it. "Daddy, please don't put me in there! Please don't, Daddy!"

"Stop whining. You are such a fucking baby! I can't stand to even look at you!" he shouts. He quickly turns my body and holds me over the pit.

I can feel the heat from the coals, and I curl my legs up to my stomach. "Please don't do it, Daddy!" I tell myself not to cry. And don't scream. 2 x 8 = . . . I can't remember. What is 2 x 8? I can't remember.

"Straighten out your legs or I'm throwing your whole body in there!" he demands.

I'm trying to straighten my legs, but it's so hot! It hurts so much I need to pull my feet away.

"If you pull your feet up one more time, I'm dropping you in!" he shouts.

16. $2 \times 8 = 16$. 2. I have two legs. Straighten my two legs. I can do this. 1 . . . 2 . . . don't pull them back. As he lowers my feet into the pit, I smell my feet burning. I start screaming and he shakes me.

"Shut up!" he screams.

I stop screaming. Stay very still. Stay very quiet. Brain, help me. 1 . . . 2 . . . 3 . . . 4 . . . 5 . . . 6 . . .

My father pulls me out and throws me to the ground. I pull my legs up to my belly and grab for my feet, but they hurt too much to touch. I'm not in the fire, but they still feel like they are burning.

"Get up and get in the car," he directs.

I hear his words, but I'm having trouble getting my legs and feet to move. I stand up but fall back down. I start crawling to the car. He comes over and yanks me by my collar to stand up. As my feet touch the rocks and sticks on the ground, my stomach feels again like it's going to throw up. I take a step and try not to think about how much it hurts. $4 \times 8 = 32$. After a couple of steps, I fall again to the ground and begin to crawl. He lets me crawl for a little ways and then makes me stand up again. After what feels like forever, I reach the car. He opens the door and I crawl onto the floor of the backseat. When we get back to the house, he drags me by my arm down the steps to the cold cellar.

I must have fallen asleep. I wake up on the floor of the cold cellar and reach for my feet in the dark. I don't know if my feet are still here. I can't really feel them. But I can touch them with my fingers, so they are there. But why can't I feel my toes moving?

I need to think about my lesson before he comes back. My lesson is to do a better job of playing with Laura. But before, he put me in the cold cellar to teach me my lesson about not playing with the kids on the playground. Am I supposed to play or not play? Ohhh. My feet hurt so much. I don't know what to do to make them not hurt. And why can't I feel my toes moving? It hurts too much to touch my feet, but I need to touch them because I can't see them, and I can't remember if they are still there or they have been burned off. Can you burn feet off someone? Oh no! What if this is only part of the lesson?

What if he wants me to burn the feet of Twinkles? What was my lesson again? Am I supposed to play or not play? My feet hurt, and I can't remember, and I can't think. I'm just going to sleep. After I sleep, I'll remember my lesson and when I wake up, I will be able to tell if my feet are still there. Just sleep, Cheri. 1 . . . 2 . . . 3 . . . 4 . . . 5 . . . 6 . . .

The remaining summer weeks in the cold cellar were a long, slow healing process for my badly burned feet. Years later in therapy, I felt very angry for how much time I lost trying to sort out the rules and lessons in a way that would make sense, all the while feeling like a failure and feeling "stupid" for not being better at keeping it all straight. With a great deal of work, I eventually came to understand that no amount of intelligence or focus could ever make sense of the craziness in the world my father had created.

CHAPTER 10

My Eyes and Ears

UNLESS SOMETHING HAPPENS to interrupt our day-to-day experiences, we come to take for granted the senses by which we experience the world. We assume, when we open our eyes in the morning, that the images of our familiar world will greet us. We immediately begin taking in sound and yet we bring our focus only to those noises that grasp our attention. There are many other noises occurring around us, but we have the magical ability to disregard any noise that does not immediately register with our brain.

My time in the cold cellar made me especially attuned to the gifts of my sight and hearing. To use the term *startling* to describe the experience of moving into a lighted room after days of complete blackness so minimizes the shock experienced by my eyes that, today, I desperately seek a better descriptor. Unless there has been an injury to our eyes, we may think of them as tired or dry, but we rarely describe an eye as hurting. But when you go from extreme, extended darkness into light, there is great pain. My eyes began to understand this experience as the norm.

I began to wear glasses at two years old, and this quickly became another demonstration of my imperfections to my father. My glasses were often kept away from me. The focus of what my eyes were doing would become another confusing puzzle for my young mind to sort out.

"Look at me when I'm talking to you!" and "Don't you dare look at me!" were often the contradictory messages I tried to decipher, to know which rule might be relevant in the moment. In a similar manner to the lemon juice in my cuts, my father would squeeze various substances (vinegar, lemon juice, mustard, onion juice) into my eyes, depending on the lesson of the moment.

Conversely, besides the lessons about what I was doing with my eyes, he taught me in my earliest years that looking into my eyes revealed so much. After all, he could look at me and tell from my eyes that I was tired, hungry, sad, angry, or whatever other emotion I was failing to hide in the moment. As a little girl, I perceived this ability as some magical quality my father had that allowed him to know everything about me because he had reminded me many times, "I am your father and I know you better than anyone in this world, so what I say about you is the truth." Eventually, in untangling the knots of this nightmare, I came to understand that if you starve a child for days, pull her out of the cold cellar and wave food in front of her face, you do not need to have magical powers to look into her eyes and know that she is hungry.

In addition, there were lessons about what other people's eyes had to endure when they saw me. From my father's perspective, having to look at me caused him and everyone else great pain. My ugliness was often too painful to be experienced and I was again banished to the cold cellar to sit in darkness and protect the world from my presence.

This sense of being a person that causes others to experience pain or discomfort simply because they have to look at you became a tough piece to sort out in therapy, years later. I remember having a conversation with a gentleman who had recently undergone throat surgery and as a result, he still had an open, gaping hole in his throat with a bandage below it that would catch bloody secretions as they drained from the wound. I remember distinctly focusing on his eyes as I noticed my stomach beginning to feel sick if I looked at the wound.

I realized I could use this experience to finally have a way to describe to my therapist how I had come to see myself and the effect

I was afraid I had on others who had to look at me. I have spent tremendous energy in trying to use a sense of humor, conversational skills, or expertise about a topic to help those who might find themselves in conversation with me, in hopes that these other attributes could distract them from the "gaping wound" sensation, in the same way I focused on that man's eyes to get through the experience.

My ears, and what I would hear, would also be a point of contention with my father, in numerous lessons about listening. In most instances, my failures were less about whether I had been really listening and more about the inability of a young child to remember an inordinate number of rules that reached far beyond her developmental abilities. I knew this because I knew with certainty that my ears were listening very intently for every sound, every intonation, any change in pitch that might be a hint as to what was expected from me in response to the most recent rant. As with every other experience, the consequences of not listening intently were severe for me or for one of our innocent pets who might have walked through the room at the wrong time.

"Cheri, get in here!" my father shouts. I jump up and run from my spot in the corner over to my father.

"Didn't you hear me call you?" he shouts.

"I'm sorry, Daddy. I didn't hear you." I feel very mad at myself for not listening more carefully, and I avoid looking at his eyes. As I look down, I see a puddle of liquid on the floor and he's holding a beer. I bet he spilled his beer and he called me to clean it up. I can do this. I know what he wants. I'll run and get a towel. I'll use that towel on that counter.

"I got it, Daddy. I'm cleaning it up." I feel proud that he didn't even have to ask me to clean it up. I know what to do and that should make up for my not hearing him the first time he called me. I feel cold beer on my head, but I'm just going to keep cleaning up this spill. He walks away and goes back to the den, and after I clean the spill, I go back to my corner. I think I got it cleaned up fast and he didn't have to ask me, so if I just listen carefully and don't miss him calling me again, we won't have to have another lesson about listening. I'll sit here, very still and quiet, and I'll be sure to hear him if he calls for me. I'll watch him closely too, and I'll see if his mouth moves and he gets ready to call me. I can get to him very quickly. I can do this.

After a while, I hear him shout, "Get me another beer!" and I run to the kitchen and bring him a beer. As I take the beer to him, I am careful not to run or trip over my brother's foot, where he is sitting on the sofa watching television. I return to my spot in the corner and I feel very satisfied that I heard him the first time he called, and I got the beer without any problem. As I continue to sit here, I start to feel sleepy. Mom went to bed a while ago with a headache. I think Yvette is in our room. She's probably reading a book. I wish I could have a book, but I know I would not listen well enough if I had a book so it's good that he won't let me have one. Maybe if I move over just a little bit, I can see what my brother is watching on TV. No, I probably should just keep watching my father in case he calls for me again. I wasn't listening very well when I missed his call earlier. It's a good thing I cleaned up the spill quickly, so he didn't get madder.

"Time for bed, Steve," my father says.

"Just a few more minutes, Dad, please?" my brother asks.

"Five minutes and then it's bed and don't ask again," my father says.

After a few minutes, Steve gets up, turns off the television and goes to bed. "Good night, Dad," he says, walking out of the room.

"Good night, son," my dad answers.

I'm probably not going to be able to sleep in my bed tonight because I didn't do a good job of listening earlier. That's OK. I understand that I did bad and he didn't even really get mad. The cold cellar will be OK, but I hope he sends me there soon. I feel sleepy and I'll be in trouble if I fall asleep here. I need to stay awake a little longer in case he calls for me again.

"Get to the cold cellar," he finally directs. I jump up, head to the basement stairs and slowly walk down. I remember the rule about not turning on the light and wasting his electricity. The cold cellar door is cracked, and I open it enough to go in. I use my hands to feel along the wall until I reach the back and slide to the ground and curl into a ball. I'm really cold, but I need to just go to sleep and not think about being cold. My brain will help me. A . . . B . . . C . . . D . . . E . . . F . . .

What is happening? I feel him grabbing my ankle and he begins to drag me across the dirt floor of the cold cellar and then onto the cement floor of the basement.

"You will learn to listen to me if it's the last thing you learn!" he shouts.

I don't understand. I was sleeping. I was in the cold cellar. He told me to go to the cold cellar. I wasn't supposed to be listening. What does he mean? Oh, wait. I remember. He called me earlier when he spilled his beer. He's right. I wasn't listening and didn't hear him call. That's why he's mad. OK, a listening lesson. I need this because I didn't hear him. I can do this lesson. I will concentrate and listen. I feel his hand grab my hair and lift me to my feet. He pulls on both of my ears.

"Do I need to tell you again what these are for?" he shouts in my left ear as he pulls hard on both ears.

It hurts, but I have to make sure my face doesn't show that it hurts. "No, Daddy. I remember. My ears are for listening. I'm sorry I didn't listen better earlier. I will listen better from now on. I promise. I will get my ears to listen better!"

He lets go of my ears. OK. I learned this lesson. I know to listen. Wait. Where is he going? What is he doing? What is he grabbing? What is he doing with Steve's baseball bat?

Owwwwww! The sharp pain that goes through the left side of my head knocks me to the floor. I grab at the side of my head. I'm screaming. I'm not supposed to, but I can't stop. My hand feels wet and I look and see blood. Where is he? I need to be quiet, but I can't stop the noise coming out of me. It's not a scream, but it needs to stay inside of me. Please, brain. Help me be quiet. Oh, my ear hurts. I can't hear. He's picking up the bat. Oh, no! I need to get away.

"Shut up! I don't want to hear another sound out of you, or I'll hit you again!" he shouts. I curl into a ball and hold the side of my head.

He throws the bat across the room and walks back up the basement steps, turning the light off as he reaches the top. He does not bother to lock me in the cold cellar. I do not move. I lie on the floor, holding my ear, hoping I can stop the bleeding and stop the hurting. The next day at the hospital, my father explains to the doctor that I got up early and was sneaking downstairs when I fell down the stairs. A misplaced toy left at the bottom of the stairs created this injury.

That day I underwent surgery on my left ear. A carefully implanted prosthesis replaced the shattered bones in my middle ear. Over the next few years, my ear easily became infected. The doctor cautioned about being very sure no water got into the ear.

In another lesson where I had apparently not been listening well, my father deliberately poured water into my ear over several days until another infection started. My mother secured the usual medicine from the doctor; however, depending on the day, my father viewed the need for medicine as a sign of weakness and some days he would toughen me up by withholding it.

On one of those days, he continued to pour water into my ear and refuse the medicine and I eventually landed in another emergency room. (We rotated around the three hospitals located about thirty miles from our town, in three different directions.) The swelling had extended down my face and into my throat. They put me in the hospital for three days and gave me IV antibiotics to counter the massive infection my body was fighting. The numerous ear infections and the need to replace the prosthesis (twice) have continuously reminded me of my lessons about listening, as I have needed eight additional ear surgeries throughout my lifetime. It has become more important for me to learn strategies to listen carefully, including reading lips, because my father's attempts to instill listening skills took away the hearing in my left ear.

CHAPTER 11

Rules

Do not ask for anything.
Do not ask for anything for anyone else.
Stay as still as possible.
Do not sit on the furniture.
Do not look at the television.
Do not play with other children.
Do not speak to anyone unless they speak to you first.

Do not look at me. (Look at me when I speak to you.)
Do not spill anything.
Do not leave crumbs on the floor.
Never wake me up when I'm sleeping. (If I'm going to be late for work, wake me up.)

Be as quiet as possible at all times.
Do not talk back.
Do not cry.
Do not yell/scream.
Do not show fear.
Do not laugh. (Laugh at my jokes.)

Do not ever let me see you smiling. (Smile every day at school. Smile at people in church and out in public.)

Do not talk to people at church, at school, or out in public.
Wear red clothing only on Tuesdays.
Wear blue clothing every Saturday.
Never wear dresses.
Do not throw up.
Do not have the hiccups.
Do not talk to your brothers and sister.
Do not argue with anyone about anything.
Do not express your opinion.
Do not have an opinion.
When called upon, describe yourself as stupid, ugly, and bad.
Do not act like you are better than anyone else.
Do not have fun unless I say you have earned it.
Do not act bored.
Call me King and ask permission from the King to do anything.
Do not snore.
Never open the refrigerator door.
Never say that a food tastes good or bad.
Do not sneeze if I am in the room.
Use only two squares of toilet paper.
Do not say if you are hot or cold.
Do not cringe or wince if you feel pain.
Do not ask to go anywhere.
Do not ask to go to the bathroom.
Do not discuss our family outside this house.
Do not repeat any of our rules to anyone outside this house.
Never say my name to anyone.
When called upon, repeat the phrase, "I love my daddy" or "I love my mommy."
Do not pet the animals.
Do not talk to the animals.

Do not fart.
Do not scratch an itch.
Be kind and friendly to everyone.
Rub lotion on my feet when I ask.
Bring me beer when I ask.
Never interrupt me.
Always do what I tell you to do without hesitation. (Think before you act.)

Bring me my newspaper every morning.
Do not pray to God until I say you are worthy of it.
Get A's on all of your school papers.
Do not show anyone your school papers.

CHAPTER 12

The Four Seasons

TIME PASSED SLOWLY in my house. The hours lost to inactivity, sitting in the corner or the cold cellar, were far too numerous for me to process, even now, in my adult mind. In his efforts to teach me lessons about being useful and productive, my father would often create menial tasks for me to complete, and these changed with the seasons of the year.

Autumn

The cooler weather begins early in Maine. It is not unusual, for those children lucky enough to participate in trick-or-treating, to have Halloween costumes large enough to wear over their snowsuits. Thus, moving from summer to winter allowed for a very short autumn season. For me, the hours of fall were as numerous as the leaves that dropped from the trees.

Removing the leaves from our backyard became the responsibility of the children. My older siblings and I were assigned a designated area to clean. Our clean-up process differed in that my older brother and sister were each given a rake to complete their tasks, but I was to pick up each leaf by hand and walk it to a trashcan placed on the side of the garage. As much as I welcomed the opportunity to be outside in the sun and fresh air, picking up one leaf at a time and walking back and forth to the garage was tedious and exhausting and would eventually steal my feelings of relief from not being stuck in the cold cellar.

My father would periodically watch to make sure I was not cheating by carrying more than one leaf at a time to the trashcan. While my siblings were often finished with their areas in an hour or two, my job dragged on from early morning until it was too dark to see the leaves I was endlessly trying to retrieve. I knew I would report back there first thing the next morning to continue the insanity. If I ever reached a point where I believed I had successfully cleared my area of every leaf, I would approach my father and meekly inform him I was ready for inspection.

I've been picking up leaves and finally feel ready to go into the house to find my father. "My area is clean, Daddy. I'm ready for your inspection," I say with a cautious sense of pride.

He stands up and I begin walking back to my designated prison yard, with my father following a few steps behind. I can feel the wind a little bit on my face. I hope no leaves have fallen while I was in the house getting Daddy. As I continue walking to my area, I study the ground to be sure there are no more leaves. Uh-oh. I see one yellow leaf. It wasn't there before, so it must have just fallen. I can get to it before he gets here. I run ahead and quickly pick up the leaf and begin walking toward the trash can.

"Stop!" my father shouts.

I stop in my tracks as he approaches me. I quickly begin my explanation: "It fell to the ground after I went to get you. I will throw it away and then my area is completely clear."

"It's OK, I'll take it for you," he says calmly.

I hand him the leaf and watch as he goes first over to my area and inspects for additional leaves and then turns to walk toward the trashcan. He looks pleased. He's smiling at me. That must mean he's happy with the job I did. I take a breath and my body relaxes just a little bit. "Perhaps you are good for something," he says. For a moment, I feel a sense of pride, but I also feel sad that there are so few things I can do to make Daddy proud of me.

I watch as he drops the leaf into the can. Then he picks up the trashcan and walks back toward me. What is he doing? My body tenses. Something is about to happen. He walks into my designated area and tips the can over, spreading hundreds of leaves all over the ground. My empty stomach begins to churn as I fight back feeling sick. I want to throw up. I want to cry. But all I can do is stare at all the leaves.

"You can practice your new skill again tomorrow, and this time be sure it really is clear before you come and get me!" he shouts as he walks back toward the house to get his dinner. Without being told, and knowing I have failed, I report directly to the cold cellar for the night. I know dinner is not an option tonight.

Winter

The winter months in Maine are long and cold. It was the one time of the year when being in the cold cellar was warmer than being outside. The lessons related to being useful during the winter months involved clearing the pathway from our driveway, up the front steps and across the porch to our front door. Most people use a shovel for snow removal, but I had to complete the task using a wooden spoon and a toy beach bucket.

After the tiny bucket was full, I would walk the snow to the back of the garage and dump it in a snowbank and then return to the front path to collect more spoons of snow. This was a tedious and tiring experience. On the days I was allowed to wear mittens, I felt as though I had been given a superpower and could conquer the world. Usually, however, my bare hands and tiny fingers carried the burden of a cold so deep it felt as though it was coming from inside my cells—a cold so intense that even in later months, when the temperature was higher, my hands stayed cold.

One particularly heavy snowstorm that led to hours of snow

removal resulted in a trip to the doctor's office with a case of frostbite on my fingers. I listened and apologized to the doctor as my father explained, "She is so stubborn! She begs to go outside to build a snowman and then we can't get her to leave her mittens on." As the doctor treated my hands, I found myself lost in the fantasy of actually being allowed to build a snowman. While this would never have happened to me as a child, I did have the joy of experiencing it with my own son, twenty or so years later.

Ian was four years old, and we were living near Syracuse, New York, where having enough snow to build snowmen was never really a problem. On this beautiful Saturday morning, my husband, Al, was out clearing a path, and Ian had his own small shovel, helping his dad. I watched from the living room window and briefly flashed back to the memories of me clearing a path with a spoon and a bucket and immediately felt grateful that history was not repeating itself.

Feeling equally determined to provide a different experience, I bundled myself up and headed outside, suggesting it was time to have some fun building a snowman. Ian was so excited and ran over to me with a snowball to use as the head.

"That's a great start," his dad said, "but we can do better." He then showed Ian how to roll the ball down the hill, making it larger and larger as it rolled. We each started working on our balls and soon we had three great snowballs, perfect for a large snowman.

"He needs a hat and nose, Mommy," Ian exclaimed.

"Well, let's go find them" I said and took him by the hand. His mittens were very wet and, as we walked into the house, I asked him if his hands were too cold. He quickly declared that they were cold, but not too cold for making snowmen. We gathered up a hat and scarf, and a carrot for the nose, of course. He looked around the kitchen and decided on red grapes for the eyes and the mouth. As we walked out to finish our snowman, I asked him to give me his hands.

As I placed a pair of dry mittens on him that I had left on the heater to get warm, I looked at his tiny, beautiful fingers. I had a vision of my little frostbitten fingers and, for an instant, a deep, painful ache penetrated through my hands. I held my son's hands tight and felt their warmth for just a moment, until he began to tug on my arm.

"Let's go, Mommy! We need to build two more snowmen, so we have a whole family that looks just like ours." Looking at my beautiful son, my hands and my heart felt so intensely warm, and I knew the memories of my childhood could never make me feel that frigid cold again.

Spring

Spring is the time of year when all that has died during the cold winter months begins to come back to life. Gradually, flowers poke their way through the thawing ground. Birds begin to come back from their southern journey. The grass begins to grow—growing grass that needs to be cut. My designated area was located conveniently behind the garage, out of the view of most neighbors. The opportunity my father gave me to search for a way to be useful in this world came with a pair of scissors and a large parcel of land with grass just waiting to be cut.

Other than the blisters that would form on my thumb and finger, this assignment was preferable to collecting leaves or spoons of snow. I got to sit in the sun and slowly chop each piece of grass. Physically, if I could tolerate the aching in my hand, it was a much easier task. I was fully aware that my father might be watching out the garage window to be sure I was staying fully engaged with my chore. Occasionally, I would catch a glimpse of him as he peeked around the corner of the garage, checking on my status. Because of his attentiveness, I was diligent in my focus. The warm sun beating down served as a constant motivation to avoid the cold cellar by being steadfast and careful in my grass cutting.

But a little girl's mind can be distracted and, on this one day, I found myself staring at a nearby tree, noticing the leaves that were beginning to grow. I knew that in a few months those leaves would become my nemesis, and I observed them with contradictory feelings—appreciation of their beauty but also hatred, at the same time.

As I look more closely, I see a bird sitting in a bird's nest. As I listen carefully, I'm sure I hear the sounds of baby birds too! I stand up and walk toward the tree to see if there really are baby birds and yes! Standing close to the tree, I can see the mommy bird feeding the babies. I'm so amazed that I forget about my job to cut the grass and don't even notice my father's presence until I feel his hand on my shoulder. I instantly feel complete and utter terror.

"What you doing, Cheri?" he asks, sounding so calm.

When he sounds this way, I know there will be a lesson. I don't answer his question but quickly turn and run back, plop to the ground, pick up my scissors and begin cutting my grass blades. He goes back to the garage and doesn't speak to me.

Later that night, my father grabs my locks of curly hair and drags me from my bed. He pulls me down both flights of stairs until we are standing in front of his workbench in the basement. Sitting on top of the bench are the bird nest and baby birds from the tree. I look at my father and see from his eyes that he is angry. I do not know where the mother bird is, but here is the nest with four beautiful baby birds. Using the same scissors, he forces me to cut up and kill each of the pretty babies. How could I have been so stupid? Why did I get up and walk to the tree? It's my fault that the birds had to die because I didn't follow the rules.

I buried the horror of this experience deep inside, to be recovered years later when I'd been engaged in watching with curiosity and excitement a similar nest in a tree just outside my therapist's office.

One day, I returned for my session, only to discover the nest and birds were gone. My therapist sadly explained that a squirrel had probably gotten them. The sobbing I did for the next hour resurrected what I had not been free to express that spring night in the basement.

Summer

Summer was an interesting time in my house. For a couple of very short months, we experienced beautiful, warm weather. For my family, that often meant a trip to a small, one-room camp we owned on a nearby lake. My family loved going to the lake—fishing, boating, and campfires were all signs of a more relaxed and enjoyable time.

My father was adamant that I had not yet grown into a person deserving of that type of enjoyable experience. I still had many lessons to learn and many changes to make before I might be worthy of fun and relaxation. Therefore, my place during those times was often within the damp and dark walls of the cold cellar. My father would have to commute into town for work and, on these occasions, he would stop by the house and give me morsels of food and a small bowl of water. Unlike during the school year, when my time relegated to the cold cellar usually was from Friday night to Monday morning or a night during the week, during the summer, the experience could be extended for two or three weeks at a time.

The toll this type of extended deprivation takes on a young child is directly proportionate to the length of years, if not decades, of therapy needed to recover. Probably the worst of these extended experiences was the very first summer I remember being in the cold cellar. It was the summer between kindergarten and first grade. I had grown accustomed to the timing and mind games needed to get through a weekend, but I was ill prepared for remaining in this abyss for weeks at a time.

At one point during that summer, my father stopped by and opened the cold cellar door to drop in some food and water. I do not know exactly how long I'd been in there, but it was at least a month because he said I had missed my sister's birthday (July 24), and I know I went into the room sometime in June. He propped the door open and gave me a shovel and bucket for me to clean up my feces from the floor. The one advantage to a limited amount of food is that it results in a limited amount of body waste; however, crawling around in any of it is a degrading and disgusting experience that I would wish no one to experience. Therefore, I was happy to do this job in the same way one might appreciate crawling into clean, fresh sheets on your bed.

After I finished, he turned on the cold water in the makeshift shower he'd rigged up in the back corner of the basement and allowed me to wash off.

My earliest memories of my father sexually abusing me started at around four years of age, but I suspect there had been a lot of inappropriate touching prior to when my memories start. I knew the privilege of this cold shower likely meant he was going to rape me, but as the water washed over the mud and dried poop caked on my body, the reason did not matter. It still felt good. My shower was brief, and my suspicions then came true. When he was done with me, he directed me back to the cold cellar.

Something inside me seemed to snap. I had learned from many harsh lessons that not obeying my father was, at the very least, unwise and at the most, incredibly dangerous. However, the idea of returning to the dingy pit of blackness was more than I could tolerate, and I simply had to fight back.

I ran to the bottom of the stairs and wrapped my arms around the post of the railing. "Please don't make me go back in there," I wailed. I began to make promises about how good I would be and how I would be fine if he just left me in the basement. Every idea that came into my head I blurted out, in hopes that I would say something that would convince him he did not have to return me to the cold cellar.

It felt like an eternity before he moved or spoke, but in reality, I suspect it was only a matter of minutes. The fury that ensued was a combination of screaming profanity about my daring to refuse his order and physical movements that happened so quickly I am not even sure of the sequence. Objects began to fly and he ripped my arms from the post with the force of an angry grown man against the weakness of six-year-old bones. He dropped me to the floor and began kicking me across the room until we reached the door of the cold cellar. With one last punt, my small body lifted from the floor and dropped into the cold cellar with a thud that would be the last sound I would hear for several days.

CHAPTER 13

The Vice

WHEN I WAS very young, holidays were a particularly challenging time for me. Children love holidays. I love holidays now in my life. But because holidays represent joy and love and fun and family, my father's ideas about me did not fit into the holidays. During many holidays, I was excluded and left in the cold cellar. Sometimes, I would get a reprieve if family members outside our immediate family came, as it would be difficult to explain my absence.

Christmas Eve, for example, was a time when we always went to my grandmother's (my father's mother's) house and I was always allowed to attend this event. When we arrived home, though, I was put in the cold cellar and, on several Christmases, remained there until the festivities had died down, a day or two after Christmas.

My father believed that if I knew anything about the plans for the holiday, it would spoil the event. He believed that if I looked at the Christmas tree it would ruin the holiday, so I had to tie a sock around my head, covering my eyes, any time I had to walk through the living room during the Christmas season. One year, I had not tied the sock tight enough and it slid down my face as I was walking through the living room. I quickly grabbed it and pushed it back up, but he had already noticed from his seat in the den. I tried to convince him that I did not look at the tree, but he did not believe me.

He grabbed the tree and dragged it out of the house, with all of the ornaments and lights still attached. My mother and little brother were in the kitchen when he went stomping through with the tree in tow. They both started crying, which only made him madder—at me, of course—for making him have to do this to the family. We had no tree that year, and the best I could do to help the family was to be sure the next year that I held the sock over my eyes and didn't trust tying it. I did not receive any presents, and any presents other people gave me (my grandmother, for example) were taken away as soon as the person was gone. Sometimes, he would keep the presents and give them to me for the short time the giver would be visiting. At other times, he threw them out or burned them—or made me do that.

June was a particularly difficult month. My birthday was, of course, the worst day of the year for my father. It had its own set of rituals that left me dreading June 2 for weeks in advance. Even later in life, I minimized my birthday as much as possible.

My birthday was followed two weeks later by Father's Day. The world almost had to stop turning to recognize the King on his special day of honor. On any given day, much of the focus was on my father's wants and needs, but on Father's Day, it was as though the world only existed to remember his greatness.

A week after Father's Day was my father's birthday, so the attention and celebration were continuous. My parents' wedding anniversary also fell during this time and, while I do not remember it being a real celebration between my father and mother, it was justification for additional opportunities to sexually abuse me—as though he needed an excuse to make that happen. While all holidays were challenging, I always experienced a sense of relief when July first came and I was still alive and functioning, because the best way for my father to celebrate and enjoy all of these events was to keep me locked away, out of sight and sound, so my presence would not interfere with his happy times.

The other holidays had similar themes of exclusion. If I saw any part of the Thanksgiving dinner in advance, it would be thrown out. I would listen from the cold cellar and imagine the Easter ham or the Thanksgiving turkey being served above me.

Yesterday was Thanksgiving. My father releases me from the cold cellar, and I sit in my spot in the den and smell the leftovers as my mother warms them for dinner. I sit in the corner, listening to the television and watching my father's every movement.

"Get me another beer and throw this can away," he barks.

I jump up because even though he didn't say my name, I know he was talking to me. I take his empty beer can and walk toward the trash can in the kitchen. When I get to the can, I notice a mostly eaten turkey leg in the garbage. I know my father can't see the trash can from where he's sitting. If I put the can next to the turkey leg, I can grab just a tiny bit of meat off the leg and eat it without him seeing me. I carefully place the can right next to the leg and sneakily tear a piece of meat from the bone and quickly put it in my mouth. It's cold, but it tastes so good. It seems like it just melted almost instantly, and the flavor is gone. I look down at the rest of the leg. Can I get some more really fast? I better not risk it. But it tasted so good. I better not. I better get his other beer quickly. I lick my finger to see if I can taste any more of the turkey. I turn away from the can and run right into my father, who is standing and watching me.

"Let me see your hands!"

I hold my hands out to him and I'm glad I just licked away any leftover turkey meat. He holds my fingers to his nose and sniffs.

"You're a thief! You stole turkey out of the garbage. I saw you do it! That turkey was not yours. You are a crook. Those dirty, stealing fingers smell just like turkey!" he yells. He grabs my arm and begins dragging me to the barn. He keeps yelling that I'm a crooked thief who would steal anything I could get my crooked little fingers on.

"I'm so sorry, Daddy! I wasn't trying to steal. I thought since it was in the garbage, I could just take a little bite. I won't do it again, I promise. I won't ever take anything out of the trash again."

"I don't believe you. You're a lying, stealing little thief. You'll use those filthy fingers to steal anything you want!"

When we get to the barn, he picks me up and sets me on his workbench. He takes my right hand and puts my pinky finger in the vice attached to the bench. He begins to twist the vice as it tightens on my finger. As he tightens it, the pain builds in my finger. I want to cry. I want to shout "ouch," but I know that would make it worse. 1 . . . 2 . . . 3 . . . 4 . . . 5 . . . 6 . . . I hear a snap and he stops twisting the vice. He takes my pinky finger out and puts my ring finger in the vice. He keeps doing this until he has broken all my fingers. My hands ache, but they started to just feel numb. I can't really feel anything, and I just sit on the workbench, staring at the floor. I must not cry. I must stay still and quiet. 1 . . . 2 . . . 3 . . .

Today, when I hold my hand up in front of me and put my fingers together, I see spaces and angles that are not normal. He believed I was a "crooked" little thief and left my fingers in a permanent state of being crooked. Sometimes, I find myself hiding my hands, and it took many years of therapy before I felt comfortable getting a manicure. But now, I see my hands as evidence of my strength. I use my crooked fingers to pet my dogs and cat, to hold the hand of a small child, or to offer a warm handshake in the wonderful experience of meeting a new friend.

As a small child, I constantly searched for logic and reason from the behaviors and explanations of my father's crazy and irrational thinking. As an adult, I now know there is no making sense of the absurd. It took a long time, but forty-five years later, when my therapist generously shared a plate of his Thanksgiving leftovers with me, I came home and sat at my table, picking up the pieces of turkey with my crooked fingers, tears streaming down my face. These were sad tears for a little girl who had ten fingers broken for taking a morsel of food out of the garbage can. They were also happy tears for an adult woman who was now eating the meal shared with her by a healthy, caring man who was helping her to heal, one small piece at a time.

CHAPTER 14

The Outhouse

OUR FAMILY'S CAMP started out with the bare minimum for us to be able to stay there for a few days at a time. It was a small, one-room cabin with no running water, toilet, or kitchen facilities. My parents' bed was propped up against the wall during the day. The children slept in a small, wooden storage shed out in the back corner behind the camp. If we were all there, it was a tight squeeze for the four of us to lie side by side each night.

My grandparents had the camp beside us, but my father's sister and her family were the ones usually using that property. Behind my grandmother's camp was an outhouse that the two families shared.

I hated the outhouse. It always smelled so bad and I worried I might fall into the hole. There was no light in the small, square room so if you had to go after sunset, it was a dark walk over and it always felt scary to go in there alone at night.

I never said that out loud, of course, because my being afraid of anything resulted in many lessons to overcome the fear, and the lessons were terrifying. For example, one time I cringed and stepped back at the sight of a mouse running across the basement floor. The next day I spent several hours lying naked in the bathtub with over a dozen mice crawling up and down my body. I have no idea where he got the mice from.

My mother has fixed us lunch. "I made a chocolate cake for dessert," she says.

I LOVE chocolate cake! I'm so excited that my father's at work today, so I get to have a piece of chocolate cake. My absolute favorite. But I better not be too excited, or it might make mom question whether she should give me some or not. I sit quietly and wait as she passes plates to my siblings. And then she does it. She gives me one too. I want to swallow it all at once before it gets taken away, but I also want to eat it very slowly so I can remember every bite. I am going to try and eat it not too fast and not too slow. It's so good and I think about the cake as I fall asleep that night in the little shed.

What is happening? The door is open, and I can see my father's shape in the shadow. He reaches over my brother and grabs my arm and pulls me into the night air.

"Did you eat chocolate cake today?" he asks.

"Yes, Daddy. I ate the piece Mommy gave me to eat. I didn't ask for it. I didn't waste any. I put my dish in the sink when I was done. I didn't ask for a second piece. I thanked Mommy for giving it to me," I say, quickly blurting out all the ways I did the right thing.

"You ate the last piece of chocolate cake! There was none left when I got home, you selfish bitch," he screams.

"I'm sorry, Daddy. I didn't know it was the last piece. I just ate what Mommy gave me. I'm so sorry, Daddy. I didn't know."

He grabs my arm and drags me down the path, screaming about how eating the last piece of cake was a shitty thing for me to do.

I just keep saying, "I'm sorry, Daddy."

"If you're going to act shitty, then you'll be treated shitty!"

This is the path to the outhouse. He's going to make me sleep in the outhouse tonight. I try to prepare my mind for sitting in the tiny outhouse building all night. When he opens the door, I smell that horrible smell of poop. I wait for him to throw me in and close the door, but instead he steps up into the tiny room with me. He opens the toilet seat that rests on top of the hole and, using my arm, lifts me down into the hole. I am standing in a pile of poop, pee and used toilet paper. Everything is so squishy and gross. Am I going to sink in over my head? Am I going to be able to breathe in here? The smell is so disgusting, and I can feel myself starting to throw up in my mouth. I want to plug my nose, but my hands are covered in poop, so I don't want to touch my face. Everything is slimy and gross. The pee and poop are all I can smell. Pieces of dirty toilet paper are floating around me. 1 . . . 2 . . . 3 . . . 4 . . . 5 . . . 6 . . .

I'm not sure how long I had to stay in there. I threw up a couple of times. I tried to use the strategies I used in the cold cellar—counting, saying the alphabet, and so on to distract myself from the stench and the gross stickiness. It was just beginning to get light when the door opened, and it was him. He had a pair of gloves on. He reached down and pulled me out. He sent me into the lake to wash up and reminded me, as we walked back to the storage shed, that I needed to learn not to be so selfish and remember that I will never deserve the first or last piece of anything.

As I told the story years later in therapy and the feelings resurfaced, I began to gag as I recalled the horrible smell and the feeling of being so disgusting I could hardly tolerate myself. Metaphorically, it was a feeling I would experience many times over, long after the feces had been washed away.

CHAPTER 15

Sexual Abuse

SEX, AT ITS best, is a loving and intimate expression of emotion be-
tween two people. Sex can also be fun, playful, and enjoyable. But at
its worst, sex is painful, humiliating, and absolutely terrifying. If you
are a young child, sex is not supposed to be part of your world. And
if it is, it's because you are being raped, assaulted, abused, molested,
or any other way of being inappropriately used to satisfy an adult's
sick and unhealthy fetishes. When this happens, it involves a level of
confusion, secretiveness, and humiliation that can take a lifetime to
sort through.

The ways that my father used sex as a tool to abuse me are numer-
ous. The messages he communicated through sexual acts he forced
me to participate in or watch were many and have taken years of
work to unravel. These messages were often contradictory: messages
of love and hate, pain and pleasure, good and bad, my salvation and
my damnation. Abusive sex is all about the power one person uses
over another. This power is magnified when it is an adult with a child.
It is unnatural and creates wounds that can heal but will absolutely
never completely go away.

The first memories I have of inappropriate sexual activity with my
father began very early. I remember him touching me between my
legs, and it struck me as odd because in all other instances my father
avoided touching me (unless it was to hit or grab me) and prohibited

others from touching me. I did not understand why that one location on my body seemed different from all other touching.

I wake up on the morning of my fifth birthday on June 2, 1967. I'm thinking about how this birthday means I'm now old enough to go to school, and an excited feeling begins to grow inside me.

I feel my father grab my arm. He pulls me from my bed and drags me to the basement. I know what this is. He told me I would need to give him all the reasons I should be allowed to live for another year, so I bet that's what he's going to ask me. I'm ready. I have reasons why I should be able to stay alive. I help my mother. I help my brothers and sister. I am nice to my grandmother. I do all of my chores. I am old enough to go to school. I take care of our pets. I am nice to people. I follow my father's directions. I try to be good all the time. If he asks me, I am ready.

"OK, Cheri. It's time. Why should you be allowed to stay alive until your sixth birthday?"

I begin my list, and he seems to be listening. He's looking at me kind of funny, though. Why is he grabbing my pajama top? Why is he taking it off me?

"Keep going. Why else?"

I'm trying to remember my reasons, but I want to understand what he's doing. Now he's taking off his shirt and pulling down my pajama bottoms. I'm not going to say anything else. Why is he taking off his pants? What's wrong with his peepee? Why is it sticking out like that? When he pees on me in the bathroom it doesn't look like that. He sees me looking at it, so I look away.

"That's a magic stick, Cheri. That's my magic stick," he says. "If you're a really good girl, it makes my magic stick happy and it gets bigger and bigger until 'surprise'—a special magic juice will spill out. You have to be really good to make the magic juice come out. Can you do that?"

I want to make Daddy happy and his magic stick happy, but I don't really like what it looks like, and Daddy seems kind of different right now. My stomach feels yucky and I just want to go back to my bed.

"Put the magic stick in your mouth, honey," my father says.

Honey. Why did he call me honey? He likes me right now. I can't breathe with this in my mouth. I don't like this. I want him to stop putting it my mouth. I can't breathe and it makes my lips hurt. It's too big for my mouth. I can't tell him to stop. I can't talk. I can't breathe. I think I'm going to fall down.

The next few minutes are confusing and uncomfortable as he pushes the magic stick in and out of my mouth, over and over. After a very long time, the "special juice" squirts into my mouth. Ohhh. Gross. I try to resist spitting it out, but it happens so automatically I can't stop it from happening.

My father gets really mad. "You little cunt. How dare you spit that out? You little bitch!" he yells as he grabs a handful of hair and drags me over to the cold cellar door.

"I'm sorry, Daddy. I was surprised and it tasted funny and I couldn't breathe, and my body just spit it out by accident. I'm sorry, Daddy. I won't do it again. I promise!"

He opens the cold cellar door and throws me in. I sit in the dark, thinking about the magic stick and the juice I spit out. School would be better. I'm five now and soon I will go to school. School will be fun. I already know my letters and numbers. A . . . B . . . C . . . D . . . E . . . F . . .

After a long time, he comes back, and when he opens the door, he is naked, and his magic stick is again sticking out. I prepare myself for another lesson on how to make the stick happy, and this time I am going to be careful not to spit out the special juice no matter how much it chokes me. But he doesn't put the magic stick into my mouth. Instead he sits in a chair and pulls me into his lap. At first, he just bounces me on his lap, but after a while he said the magic stick is cold and it can only get warm if I sit on it and put it inside me.

87

The excruciating pain I feel in the next few minutes is beyond the words I can find to describe it. I feel like I've been split in half. I look down and see blood between my legs. Did Daddy decide I don't deserve to live another year? I remember what it's like watching animals die and hearing them cry in pain. As my father lifts me and pushes me back down on to his magic stick over and over, I wonder, if I started counting, how far I would get before I died just like the animals.

When my father was done, he carried me to the cold cellar. He often pulled me, slapped me, kicked me from one place to another, but he had never carried me before. There was a strange moment of confusion as he gently placed me on the cold cellar floor and smiled as he looked at me and told me we now had a good reason for me to stay alive another year. He closed the door behind him, and I was left literally in a pool of blood and my mind racing with bewilderment as I felt the extreme physical pain while noticing my father had just been a little bit nice to me. The mixed messages had begun and would continue for several years.

When my father's magic stick wanted attention, I became someone my father could tolerate. I could still see the hatred for me in his eyes, but it seemed in these moments to be just a little bit softer. However, the experiences of rape continued to be agonizingly painful and often frustrating for my father. A five-year-old body is not meant to match with the sex organs of a grown man, so there were many attempts that only angered and frustrated him. As good as I was at being still and quiet in my corner, I struggled in sexual encounters as the weight of his body, the size of his penis, the smells and tastes—all of it was overwhelming and led to me not being as cooperative as he would have liked. This led to lessons and punishments. I hated these experiences, and the rare moments when he seemed to be just a little nicer or a little gentler did not sufficiently counter the anguish.

One of my father's greatest requests was for me to lie very still.

My body would often resist by turning or pulling away, so we had to engage in lessons on learning to be very still. These particular lessons took place in my bed after everyone was asleep. My father would come into my room and remove my pajamas. I would lie on my back and he would take two fishhooks and insert one into each side of my labia. He then took fishing line and tied one end to the fishhook while securing the other end to the side of my bed frame. If I moved at all, the fishhook would pull and tear. I learned how to lie very still on my back, even when my body was feeling pain.

I would be reminded of these lessons in the days to follow because whenever I peed the urine would reach the fishhook wounds and sting in a way that was similar to my earlier lessons of lemon juice in the cuts of my palms. Ironically, making the connection to my earlier lessons with pain allowed me to know I could conquer this challenge too, and the next time he came in with the fishhooks, I was ready. I did not move at all and fell asleep with a strange sense of pride for my accomplishment. I never understood the point of this lesson in staying still because as soon as the sexual act started, he moved up and down, back and forth, and in and out with a sense of urgency that seemed to negate all that I had learned about being still and quiet. Another in a long list of contradictory messages.

My father frequently cheated on my mother. Beyond raping me, he had more girlfriends in his life than I can possibly remember. Some of these women were people my mother knew, and some were not. I never heard any discussion about this between my mother and father, but I always felt like his having sex with other women was simply another thing my mother had to tolerate without question.

When I got a little older, I remember walking with my mother to a local hotel restaurant where she would meet with her friend for a morning coffee. It did not happen often, but I loved it when I was included on this adventure. However, sometimes my father would be in the same restaurant, sitting at the counter, drinking coffee. We never acknowledged each other, and he never spoke to my mother. We were only a few feet away, but we behaved as though we were all total strangers.

I thought it was even more unusual because the very nice waitress that put an extra marshmallow in my hot chocolate was also one of my father's girlfriends. She would stand at the counter and talk with my dad and then walk over to our table and be very nice to my mom, and my mom to her, as she refilled her cup of coffee. I still do not know who knew what, but I found the whole experience another confusing puzzle to ponder, then and years later, as I tried to make sense of the nonsensible.

I knew this particular girlfriend because years earlier, my father had taken me with him when he went to meet up with her. He used her and a few others to teach me how to be better at having sex with my father. Occasionally when he tried this, the woman would protest and refuse to have sex with him until I was locked in another room, but surprisingly, more of them went along with my father's request.

Watching my father have this effect on people added to the now very strong feeling that my father was normal and a well-liked, really good person, and I was the horrible, problem child that needed to be fixed. Years later in my therapy, I would wonder how so many people could have gone along with what was happening to me or could have been so willing to look the other way. I have spent a lifetime in the field of education, hoping to build awareness among teachers or use my own instincts to identify and stop abusive behaviors.

We have made great progress on this issue and, just when I think a situation like mine could never happen now, there is another horrific news story where someone was placed in an insufferable, abusive environment for years at a time. Back in the sixties in my hometown, there were several women, this waitress included, who did not appear to have a problem including a six-year-old in their sexual activities.

I never liked it, even when the woman was exceedingly nice and gentle. Sometimes, I was just supposed to stand or sit and watch. Other times I was invited onto the bed and the woman would take my hand in hers to guide what I was supposed to do. I ALWAYS felt uncomfortable and embarrassed, without having a clear understanding of what I was embarrassed about. Given that this behavior was considered normal in my world, it's confusing to me how I knew that this was something to be ashamed of. That realization later became a strong tool in helping me learn that I can trust my gut and my natural instincts.

In my awkwardness, I often would try to turn away or at least stare at the floor or ceiling, but if I got caught looking away, it angered my father, and the consequences were severe for me and sometimes for the woman he was with. I began to learn to watch without seeing. I would fix my eyes on what was happening in front of me, but in my mind, I would see another place. These early experiences led to my abilities to dissociate from the moment and put myself somewhere else—anywhere but here, watching my father's magic stick squirt special juice all over this woman's chest.

In addition to using me in sexual situations with women, my father also used me with his male friends. Similar to the times with the women, a few men objected, but several of his friends were very willing, often in their drunken states, to include me in their festivities. The housewarming incident when I was four was the introduction to my involvement with his friends, and similar scenarios were repeated for several years. Unlike the times with my father's girlfriends, there were usually a few people present instead of just the one woman and my father.

Obviously, at this point, my father viewed me as just an object and not a person, but it seemed to carry additional feelings for me that he wanted to share me with other people. I suppose in other situations that might happen in a normal family—a father asking his little girl to sing a song or share a paper from school would create a sense of pride in the child that her father was anxious to share her accomplishments with his friends. In this situation, his willingness to share me in sexual activities never created a feeling of pride. I continued to be embarrassed and uncomfortable.

Often, the men would take me behind the furnace to the back corner of the basement and, at these times, I had an odd sense of abandonment by my father. This became a point of confusion in my therapy, as my father was never a protector for me. In reality, he was often the instigator of my pain and abuse, but somehow, his allowing someone else to do the same thing to me felt like an even bigger betrayal. Several of my father's friends were smokers and they all smelled of alcohol. I found their magic sticks just as disgusting as my father's and this created negative images and experiences that made healthy relationships with men later in life an extraordinary challenge.

On one particular evening, I had a rare incident of becoming aggressive. I had already been exposed to two of his friends' requests, and I was now with a third man. I felt as though I just could not participate any longer. I can't remember if it was an accident or intentional, but I bit the man's penis. He screamed with pain and began yelling. He pulled away from me and continued to yell at my father as he stumbled over his pants, which were around his ankles, causing him to fall to the floor. All of the men began to laugh, and I did too.

My father was laughing too—for just a few seconds. Then the rage took over. He came over and kicked me in the mouth. Two of my front teeth were lost, somewhere in the blood spilling from my mouth. In the next few minutes, I made apologies to the man I bit and promises to my father and his friends that I would never do such a thing again. It took many years of therapy before I could admit that I really wanted to bite off every one of their magic sticks and shove them in my father's meat grinder.

CHAPTER 16

The Sexual Abuse Gets Worse

BECAUSE MY MEMORIES have always been very present to me, I have not had a lot of experiences with recovering a new memory. My focus has been about recovering the feelings that were so deeply buried with each memory. But fifteen years into my therapy, I was caught off guard when I did remember new information, and it was related to the sexual abuse experiences I had with my father.

I knew my father had sexually abused me for years, and I had some very specific memories of incidents like those I have shared, but I did not have an abundance of memories, considering the frequency with which the sexual abuse occurred. I often just referred to my father having raped me without really filling in any details.

One time while in a Skype session with my therapist, we were talking, not really about sex but about dying. My therapist had recently been away and, during times he was away for vacations or other reasons, I would experience periods of extreme terror. We had been working for years to sort out why this was so much stronger when we separated for a vacation than when we separated naturally in our regular schedule. I was trying to describe how strong the sensation was when he was gone that I was absolutely certain I was going to die. We had explored this issue before and attributed these feelings to concerns about starving to death in the cold cellar, dying from not having enough water, or even the idea that the house would catch on fire while I was locked in the cold cellar and no one would know I was there, to save me. All of these were reasonable explanations for my extreme terror when separating, but even with the usual processing and emoting, the feelings would not subside.

Over time, I learned that I can identify when a puzzle piece fits and when we are a little off and an issue is still not quite right. This problem with separating is one of those situations. I had a sense that there was something more, but we could not seem to figure it out. In this particular Skype session, my therapist asked a simple question: "How are you going to die?"

I thought about it for a minute and began having flashes of memories. Apparently, as my therapist later described it, I began holding my throat. I could feel my throat closing up. I kept saying I couldn't breathe. I went into a full-blown panic attack, which was not one of my responses in my therapy work. I kept pulling at my throat as though something needed to be removed and in reality, there was nothing around my throat and nothing was impeding my breathing. I told him I thought I was going to pass out.

He calmly assured me that, if that should happen, I would just begin breathing again and that I would be fine. He encouraged me to tell him what I was seeing and what was happening. It became very clear to me. My father was choking me. He was raping me and the more aroused he became the more he tightened his grip on my throat. He was holding me by my neck as he moved me up and down on his penis. As he got closer to an orgasm, he squeezed tighter, until everything went black.

After this memory, I had a bunch more memories of him choking me during sex with his belt, a rope, a tie, and numerous other objects. I remembered being suspended by my throat, much like a hanging, while my father slammed up against me, increasing his arousal. In these memories, my father was not being pleasant or nice. He was angry and hostile. He was hurting me, and the more he hurt me, the more aroused he became until he reached his orgasm. I believed with tremendous certainty that this was how I was going to die.

It took many sessions to process all of this, and it was painful to remember. In my mind, I had created a scenario where my father hated me except when he was interested in sex. Although I would not stretch it to believe he loved me, I did associate his only positive feelings toward me with the times he raped me. I held on tightly to these beliefs, and it was only after allowing the real memories to surface that I was forced to face the reality that there was never anything my father liked about me.

This may seem obvious to anyone learning about these experiences, but to a little girl who desperately wanted to be loved by her father, she held onto the false belief that at least in one way he liked her. It took fifty-six years and the recollection of these violent and hateful memories to show me the truth and allow me to finally give up the fantasy of hoping that my father loved me in some way.

Surprisingly, once I came to understand that experience, I also could see my father in a much more accurate way, allowing me for the first time to finally hold him totally accountable for the horrors of my childhood. Up until then, I knew it was his fault, but I believed I shared in some of the responsibility. Once I have the real-life pictures in my head of a man being so aggressively violent with a little girl to satisfy his sexual urges, I no longer need to want someone like that to love me. I am also willing to give up any blame or responsibility. This puzzle piece has painfully, but rewardingly, fallen into place.

CHAPTER 17

Uncle Bub

I NEVER KNEW my mother's father. He died of a heart attack at age forty-four, when my mother was eighteen years old. Her mother was one of my favorite family members. I loved my grandmother very much, and as I got older and my father was less present in the family, I got to see her more. I remember staying at her apartment sometimes and watching her favorite show on Saturday night—*The Lawrence Welk Show*. She also invited me over whenever the Miss USA Pageant was on, but we both usually fell asleep before the winner was crowned. My grandmother died when I was sixteen, but I have fond memories of us playing Yahtzee and Rack-O whenever I visited.

Later, when I left college and returned to my hometown to do my student teaching, I rented the same apartment my grandmother had lived in when I used to visit her. It felt good to live in an apartment that already had good memories, and I stayed there until I married a year later and moved to Florida with my husband, Al.

My mother had one brother, Ronald, who we called Uncle Bub. Uncle Bub was very well liked by all the children in the family. Although he and his family lived in New Hampshire, we would get together a couple of times a year. I loved those visits because his daughter, Melody, was born two weeks before me and we grew up not only as cousins, but as best friends. Whenever we got together, my father seemed to forget all the rules, and as long as we stayed out of his way, he let me play with Mel and he never talked about the cold cellar. Usually, after the visit, I would have to do some sort of penance and show deep gratitude to him for allowing me to play and participate with the family, but it still made it worth it to have those experiences.

Uncle Bub was very generous with his time with the children. We could often talk him into leaving the adults behind and taking us to the movies or mini-golf or just to go for a ride in his station wagon, stopping for an ice cream along the way. I remember my grandmother sometimes expressing concern about the kids needing to leave him alone and let him visit with the adults, but that didn't stop us from begging for the next adventure.

Uncle Bub was a musician, and some of my fondest memories were the visits to his house in New Hampshire, where he would play the piano while we engaged in a group singalong that lasted until the wee hours of the morning. Because he was a musician, he often worked until three or four in the morning and then would sleep until noon the next day. We would anxiously wait for him to get up to take us to the beach or for an ice cream. It was always a fun time when my aunt would announce we could go in and wake up Uncle Bub. On one of my visits to Uncle Bub's house, when I was nine years old, I was the one who woke him up.

"Cheri, would you like to go wake up Uncle Bub?" my aunt asks.

"Yes, please!" I answer with enthusiasm. I run to his room with excitement.

I see him lying on his side, facing the wall. I want to wake him up, but I don't want to scare him. I reach up and put my hand on his shoulder. "Wake up, Uncle Bub! It's time to get up. Maybe we could go for a ride?"

He slowly rolls over and smiles at me. I love that Uncle Bub likes me and he never treats me like my father does. He doesn't necessarily treat me special, but he treats me like all the other kids and he's nice to all of us.

"Climb up on the bed and tell me everything I've missed so far this morning," he says.

Without hesitation, I crawl up and start talking to him about the morning. "Mel and I have been playing in her room, and then Aunt Ev made us pancakes, and now we're doing the dishes, but Aunt Ev told me I could come wake you up. Mel says we should go for a ride. Can we go for a ride?"

As I sit next to him talking, he pulls me down next to him and starts playing with my curly hair. "Your curls are so beautiful, Cheri. I love your hair," he tells me. My father hated my curls and they were often a source of fury with him, so in this moment I'm feeling very happy that Uncle Bub actually likes my curls.

As I finish my story about the morning, I sit up, exclaiming, "I'm going to go dry the dishes so we can be ready to go. Hurry and get up!"

I feel his hand grasp my upper arm and pull me back down. "Stay for a few more minutes, Cheri."

I try to pull away, but he doesn't let go. I want to leave, but I don't want to make my uncle mad. He's so nice to me. I guess I could stay a little longer. I will just count to sixty and then leave. 1 . . . 2 . . . 3 . . . 4 . . . 5 . . . 6 . . .

"You want me to take you to the beach?" he asks.

"Yes!"

"Well then, stay here and keep me company for a few more minutes. Here, curl up next to me, under the covers."

I feel my stomach getting hot. I always have such a good time with Uncle Bub, so I'm confused about what's happening now as his voice gets sterner and more forceful, directing me to get under the covers and lie next to him. I become very still and follow his directions. He begins to rub my stomach on top of my shirt and then untucks my shirt from my pants and begins rubbing my stomach and chest. His hand slides down and unzips my pants, and his fingers reach between my legs. I feel frozen and I stare at the ceiling, trying to become invisible.

After some time of him rubbing between my legs with one hand and touching himself with his other, my aunt hollers from the other room and shouts for Ronald to get out of bed and for me to come get some lunch. As if on cue, I pull myself away, zip up my pants and run out of the room.

I later learn that my uncle had gotten in trouble several times before this incident with me, and several times after, for inappropriately touching children and one disabled adult. As with all of my other experiences, no one in the family ever talked about this behavior as being wrong or inappropriate, and I once again felt as though I had done something wrong. After all, I was excited to go wake him up and I felt really good when he smiled at me and gave me his attention. I must have communicated to him that I wanted him to touch me like that. I did, however, stop asking to go places with him, and from that point forward tried to keep my distance.

Later, when we were adults, my sister shared her experience with my uncle taking her bra off and chasing her as she tried to get away from him touching her breasts. Compared to the painful and hurtful abuse of my father, this treatment by my uncle felt like no big deal, and it wasn't until years later that I recovered appropriate feelings of anger and betrayal toward him.

It was challenging to figure out what normal was in such an abnormal family. I have many unanswered questions about my mother. In my therapy, there was such a focus on my father's obvious issues that my mother got lost in all of it. I've always said that, as a woman who never worked or drove a car and relied entirely on a man for support, she simply did the best she could. Knowing that her brother had inappropriate sexual experiences with me, my sister, and other children has made me realize that my mother likely also experienced sexual abuse by her brother. This experience must have led her to being with a man like my father, but it's unlikely the stories and questions around that will ever be clear. My hope is that my generation can be the one that breaks the cycle of abuse and craziness from both my father's and mother's sides of the family.

CHAPTER 18

My Pregnancy

WHEN I WAS ten years old, I started my period. Ironically, just two weeks earlier, one of my friends' older sisters had started her period and my mother chose to tell me about it. I was grateful because I believe I would have been quite concerned had I not had that earlier conversation.

At this point, my father was raping me far less frequently. He was absent from the house a lot more and spent most of his time with his friends and girlfriends and usually did not include me. Perhaps it was getting harder to cover things up. Perhaps my getting older made him more cautious about what I might say. Or perhaps he just did not care enough about me anymore to even bother to hate me.

I was happy to have less focus on me. I could now sit on the furniture and participate in life in a different, but limited way. A couple of months after starting my period, it suddenly stopped. My mom explained it sometimes worked that way, but when I started gaining weight, she took me to see Dr. Teagan.

Around ten o'clock that night, my father came and got me out of bed. Although it happened far less frequently, I still was banished to the cold cellar on random nights, and I thought perhaps this was one of those nights. Instead, we got into my father's truck. I knew better than to ask where we were going, so I just sat quietly, and we rode for a long time.

At one point, I fall asleep and awaken to my father shaking my arm. "Wake up, Cheri. We're almost to the doctor's office," he says.

"What doctor?"

"You don't know him. It's a doctor here in Portland that's going to help us out."

"Help us out with what? Are you sick? Am I sick? What's going on?"

"Dr. Teagan says you're pregnant, and this doctor is going to take care of the problem."

My mind starts whirling. What the hell? I'm pregnant. I have a baby inside of me? Is it a baby boy or a baby girl? How could I have a baby inside of me and not know it? I have so many questions, but I look over at my dad, and I can tell it's best for me to be as still and quiet as possible.

He takes me in through the back door of this tall building. There's a doctor and a nurse and my father and me—I don't see any other people. The doctor is quick and matter of fact. "This might feel un-comfortable, but you'll be fine. It will only take about ten minutes."

The nurse tells me to take off all my clothes and lie down on a hard bed covered in white sheets. She puts another sheet over me. I wish I had a pillow. Even though I'm used to the cold, this room feels especially frigid.

"What's the doctor going to do?" I ask. "Is it going to hurt?"

The nurse responds harshly, "He's going to fix your life and it might hurt, but you should have thought about that before you had sex."

I don't remember much about the abortion itself, other than how loud the suctioning machine was and how no one looked at me. I lay on the bed and stared at the ceiling, wondering if the baby was a boy or a girl and if it would hurt when the doctor took it out. After just a few minutes, the doctor stood up and left the room. The nurse told me to lie still and warned me that I might feel some cramps. I fell asleep and woke up when the nurse came in a while later.

She lectured me about being too young to be having sex with boys and said I needed to stop doing that immediately. She told me never to talk about this doctor's visit with my friends or anyone else. I was to go home and rest in bed for a couple of days and then go back to school and forget about it.

It was a long time later that I heard the word *abortion* and learned more about what had been done that night. Sometimes, I think about the fact that I only knew I had a baby in my stomach for a few minutes before it was gone, but years later, in therapy, I cried some of the same tears as though it was one of the kittens or bunnies that I'd loved and had to kill. My father drove me home and told me the same thing the nurse did—don't tell anyone about this night. He never again touched me in a sexual way, and I never talked about it until it was safe, a long time later.

As a result of these many experiences, sex has been a difficult and complicated reality for me. Long after that trip to Portland in the middle of the night, my father's messages, images, and experiences have wakened me out of a deep sleep and destroyed many other nights for me. My confusion made me a target for others who want to treat me as an object to satisfy their needs.

This treatment became such a common occurrence for me that my therapist had to do a reality check with me years later, when I shared a story with him about my mother. I was sixteen and living on my own. I had my own car, so I drove the hour to see my mother where she'd been living for a couple of years, with her new husband and my brother. We were sitting at her kitchen table and I was talking to her about school and about my frequent babysitting opportunities. I shared with her how much I love children. She shared with me that she wished she could have another child. I was a little surprised by this, and I guess she could read that on my face because she continued by saying that her new husband really wanted to have another child and she felt badly that she was too old to give him one. She felt a little uncertain about her marriage and wished she could solidify it by giving him a baby.

She then asked me if there was any possibility that I would consider having a baby for her. I told her I didn't think I would like having sex with Bill, and she said it would be over quickly and because I was so young I would probably get pregnant the first time. She started to cry, and I could hear the familiar desperateness in her voice whenever she worried about whether she could keep the man in her life happy with her. I told her I would need to think about it.

I had pretty much decided to say yes to her but happened to mention it while walking with my father's sister, and she was adamant that I should not do this. After a lot more thought, I called my mom a few weeks later and said I was very sorry to disappoint her, but I just could not do it. Although I was feeling tremendously guilty for saying no, she said it was fine and we went back to talking about the weather and it was never mentioned again.

As I told this story years later to my therapist, he pointed out how casually I had treated the idea that my mother had asked me to have sex with her husband and give birth to a baby for her. I immediately began to defend my mom and tried to get him to see how important it was to her to try to please her husband, and it was only from this place of wanting to make him happy that she would have asked me to do this. It took many months before I could see that this whole scene was very far removed from normal. In my mind, if I had something to offer that could help someone, then of course I had to do it (regardless of the impact on me) because doing it might make up for my underlying badness and make it OK for me to be taking up space here on earth. When a human is treated as an object, it takes a long time and a great deal of work to begin to feel like a person who does not have to earn the air they breathe.

CHAPTER 19

Homeless

WHEN I WAS fifteen, my parents divorced. My mother had taken a job cleaning rooms at a local motel before the divorce. Shortly after the divorce, my mother met one of her co-worker's brothers and months later, she remarried.

My father had moved to the camp and was living there. My sister, Yvette, and my older brother, Steve, had moved out on their own. My younger brother, Paul, and I were left with my mother. My mother's new husband, Bill, lived about ninety minutes away in a small mobile home. He told my mother that he did not have room for her to bring both my younger brother and me to live with him. Because my brother was only twelve, she chose to take him with her.

This actually was OK with me because I wanted to stay and graduate from my current high school. The plan was that I would stay with different friends, but I essentially became homeless. I did stay with friends—sometimes for a weekend and at other times for a month or so. I lived for a short time with Yvette.

My father, when he felt I deserved it, paid the one hundred dollar monthly child support payment directly to me, and I offered it to the people I would stay with as compensation for any trouble I might be bringing to their lives. Often, I could sense I was an intrusion to the families who let me sleep on their couch or in their basement, so I continued trying to be as still and quiet and invisible as possible.

The Penobscot River ran through our town and I always loved being near water. To this day, water calms me and brings me peace as it did back then. So, often, I would find myself sleeping under the bridge that connected our town to a small island. I felt safe under the bridge and I could just watch the water until I fell asleep. Additionally, I was not being a problem or inconvenience to anyone when I was under the bridge.

At sixteen, I purchased a yellow '65 Dodge Dart with money I had earned and saved from babysitting, and that became my real sense of home. I was fortunate to have many people willing to take me in or help me out during that time. In the warmer months, I would often sleep in my car, but in Maine, there are not many warm months. The custodian at the high school was a wonderful man who would often leave the locker room door ajar for me so I could sneak in there to sleep on really cold nights and get a fresh shower when I needed it.

In October of my senior year of high school, a married couple, who were both English teachers at my school, offered to let me live with them, and I remained there until I left for college the following August. Eleven months does not sound like much time, but I would not be here today if they had not taken me in and given me the gift of living in a happy, healthy, stable home. Even though it was for less than a year of my life, their kindness, their normalcy, and their love allowed me to catch my breath from everything I had experienced in my first seventeen years. I could then take that energy, think about a future, and believe my life could be different. I left that environment with wounds starting to heal and enough confidence to put myself through college and ultimately choose the path of my life.

During this time of homelessness, I had a small dog, Billie, who went with me everywhere. She was a wonderful companion and kept me company on whatever couch I was on or curled up under the bridge with me. It is challenging to describe how insignificant I felt when I slept in places where I felt like I never belonged. But Billie always kept me focused and grounded. When I felt like I mattered to no one, she would curl up in my lap and lick my face, reminding me

I definitely mattered to her.

One winter holiday, I found myself with no place to stay. The school was locked and many of my friends had gone away for the week. It was especially cold, and staying outside was not an option, as I knew both Billie and I would be in danger of freezing to death.

The family camp we had at a nearby lake had burned to the ground, and my father was rebuilding the one-room cabin into a beautiful two-story, three-bedroom home. As you can imagine, I had no desire to go there, but I truly felt I had no options. So, Billie and I hitchhiked and walked our way the ten miles to my father's house. He agreed to let me stay for the week for an agreed upon twenty-five dollars of my child support money. I hoped that he would be at work or sleeping most of the time, and I felt relieved that I would not be out in the cold for the next few days.

Money was very tight for me. During the summer months, I worked at a local dairy bar, but during the winter months, my only source of income was babysitting. I loved babysitting because I loved children. I had over thirty families that would regularly use me for babysitting, and often they would allow me to sleep at their house the night I was sitting for them, so this helped a great deal from a practical perspective.

I had a babysitting job the Saturday at the end of the week I was staying at my father's house. When I got home from the job, I walked into my father's house, and he was sitting at the table eating his dinner. I looked under the table to greet Billie because that's where she would be if someone was at the table eating, and she was not there. My father had recently installed a large sliding glass door with even larger windows on each side of the door, providing for a beautiful and expansive view of the lake from the living room. I walked over, thinking that Billie must be outside, but when I slid the door open and called for her, she did not come.

"She's not here!" my father yelled.

It had been eight or nine years since my father had done anything with an animal, but in that moment my heart seemed to stop, and flashes of horrible memories came flooding back. My father told me to look down at the glass door and when I did, all the air left my body and I could not breathe as I saw the chew marks on the casing of the newly installed sliding door.

"I took her to the shelter in Bangor and told them to put her down," my father explained. "I told them she was violent and had bitten two people and she needed to be put to sleep."

I ran to the phone book and began searching for the number. I called, but it was Saturday evening and they were closed. I could only hope I could reach them in time. The next morning, I left my father's house and hitchhiked and walked the twenty miles to Bangor. It was dark when I arrived and the shelter was closed, but I searched through the windows and listened carefully to try and recognize Billie's bark. I slept under a rug outside one of the kennels and was waiting there when they opened Monday morning. The person who got there first was very kind but explained that Billie had already been put to sleep.

It may seem odd to say this, given the history of my experiences earlier in life, but in that moment, I honestly felt the most broken I had ever been. I walked away from the shelter and did not even know what direction to go. My heart was in pieces and the loneliness washed over me like a tsunami.

Without any awareness or planning, I made my way back to my hometown and found the locker room door ajar, since school was now back in session. The custodian had saved me once again. As he had done several times in the past, he had left some food in my locker, along with a note. "Didn't see you today. Someone left a box. It's in the first shower stall. Stay warm."

I went to the shower stall and found a box with the few items of clothing I had left at my father's house. He had put my child support check in the box as well. The check was written for ten dollars and included a piece of paper indicating twenty-five dollars had been subtracted for one week's rent and sixty-five dollars for the shelter's fee to put Billie to sleep. The note also said there would be no payment for the next three months to cover the cost of the repair to the door. The last item in the box was Billie's blue dog collar. I slowly walked back to my locker and got out my peanut butter sandwich and my books to begin reading the assignments I'd missed that day. As I held Billie's collar in my hand, my heart felt so heavy I had to work just to keep breathing.

CHAPTER **20**

High School Chemistry

I ALWAYS LOVED going to school. No real surprise there, given what my home life was like, but I also always enjoyed the focus and attention that school created. I could put my energy into working on an assignment and, for a brief time, my brain could rest from the issues of pain, vigilance, and survival.

It is no coincidence that I have now spent thirty-six years of my adult life working in schools. I feel comfortable in schools. In my roles as a classroom teacher, a school counselor, and a school principal, I have experienced many moments of true joy in watching children and adults in the learning environment.

I was very fortunate in fifth grade that my teacher, Mrs. Dodge, recognized my love of children and allowed me to spend every Friday afternoon going to the kindergarten classes and reading to the children. Somehow, Mrs. Dodge was wise enough not to mention this to my parents, as if she knew the privilege would be taken away if they learned of my special Friday afternoon adventures.

When I went into sixth grade the following year, Mrs. Dodge let my middle school know about my love of working with children. My wonderful school counselor, Charlie, made special arrangements for me to go to a nearby preschool on Tuesday and Thursday afternoons to work with the three-, four-, and five-year-old children. There was never a concern that I would not keep up with my classes, and the joy

I got from going to the New Alderbrook Nursery School motivated me to be as close to a perfect student as possible.

The owners of the nursery school, Pat and Ed Ranzoni, welcomed me without question. I do not know what explanation they were given as to why I was out of school two days a week to come to their nursery school. It may have been as simple as to nurture my love of children, but I suspect there was at least an implication that I was also child who could benefit from being in a loving and accepting environment.

Both Pat and Ed were gentle, loving, and fun with the children. As I watched Ed engage in such a positive way, I became aware of a distant sadness deep within me and found myself secretly keeping him in my sights as I moved around the rooms, playing and reading with the children. I liked hearing his voice and watching his kind and gentle nature, even when correcting a child's behavior. When he sat on the floor with three kids in his lap, reading them a story, I had to focus on the playdough activity I was doing with a child to keep myself from running over to sit in his lap too. The days at this school began to help me understand that there was another way of being with children that did not include painful lessons, humiliation, and constant rage.

During my time there, Pat attended a Saturday training, and she invited me to go and paid the additional registration fee so I could attend. I do not remember everything that day, except that I was one of the youngest participants and wanted to soak up everything I could about children and learning. One session I attended was about using imagination when playing with young children. They modeled and had us participate in some imaginary journeys.

The next week, when I went to the nursery school, Pat and Ed helped me set up for teaching my first lesson. We arranged the small chairs in a circle and I nervously helped the children buckle their seat belts as I guided all of them on an airplane ride over our town. We pretended to look down on each of our houses and noticed the horses playing in the field near our nursery school from above. The children shouted out details of what they were seeing below them, all while sitting in a chair in the middle of the classroom.

As a twelve-year-old girl facilitating the excitement of this activity with a group of four- and five-year-old children, I knew my love of children and learning were being etched in stone. Later, while working on my bachelor's degree in Child Development and Family Relations, I learned more about the value of imagination and realized that my imagination may very well have been what saved me in those many hours of isolation in the cold cellar.

School continued to be an escape for me, and I loved it. I loved my own classes, and I loved the opportunity to work with younger children in their classes. I admired my teachers and craved their love and attention from a distance. I still carried with me a desire to be close and an urgency to stay away. I watched them from playground corners and backs of classrooms. While I appreciated the relationships with my peers, my interest and attention were always on the adult teachers.

This interest surfaced even further with the few male teachers I had along the way. The lack of love and attention from my father had left me hungry for positive male attention, and I would seek it out in healthy and unhealthy ways throughout my life, until much later, when I began to understand the pattern.

One such attraction was with my high school chemistry teacher, Mr. Sulya. He had a quiet style with his students but often used his sense of humor in his interactions. I really liked that, and I liked it when he would joke with me. In my senior year, I had Mr. Sulya for a double lab class and also as my homeroom teacher, so I saw him several times a day. He always stood at the front door of the classroom as classes were changing and I made it a point to enter through that door, passing right by him while many other students just slipped into class via the back door. I was quiet and "invisible" but still watched him carefully, laughed at his jokes, and made sure I did well in his class.

I was beyond excited when he selected me from several volunteers to be his assistant and stay after school to help wash the beakers and other lab equipment. This became one of my favorite parts of the day. After a couple of weeks, I began to feel more comfortable and easily engaged with his joking and began to share information with him about my day. I started staying longer after finishing the cleaning and I would sit in a big easy chair he had next to his desk to do my homework, while he worked beside me at his desk.

One afternoon, as I sat in the chair beside him, he began talking about how stressed he was. He said that his wife had had a hysterectomy a couple of weeks before. He laughed as he talked about how not getting any sex was really putting him in a bad mood. As he was talking, he reached over, placed his right hand on my breast, and squeezed. He talked about what a good assistant I had been in the lab and asked if I would like to become his favorite assistant and help him feel better by relieving his stress. He moved his hand from my breast and slid it down over my stomach to between my legs. His left hand was rubbing on his crotch.

I did not say no. I did not say yes. I said nothing as my insides caught fire and I froze, trying to be as still and quiet and as invisible as possible. He got up, took my hand, and suggested we go into the closet. He pulled me to my feet and walked ahead of me into the closet. Instead of following him, I went running out of the room.

I ran to the room of the English teacher I was now staying with and asked if she was ready to go home. I was silent all the way home and all through dinner. Eventually, in a slow and careful way, I told Jeanette and Phil what had happened. I was embarrassed. I was sure it was my fault because I knew inside that I was enjoying his attention, so I must have communicated that I wanted to have sex with him.

I was afraid he would be mad at me for leaving. I felt guilty that after he had picked me from the volunteers, I had let him down and not given him what he wanted. The next day, with my permission, Jeanette and Phil reported the incident to the guidance counselor. The guidance counselor at my high school was now Ed Ranzoni—the New Alderbrook Nursery School had closed, and this was Ed's new job. I talked with Ed about what had happened and then he called Mr. Sulya in to talk with the two of us.

Sadly, school personnel are much more educated about the protocol for such experiences today, because of the frequency of these events over the years, but back then, no one was quite sure how to proceed. So, I sat in this small office with two men who each had represented something very important to me. The room felt as small as the cold cellar, and Mr. Sulya's chair was inches from mine as Ed sat across from us behind his desk, facilitating the very uncomfortable conversation that followed.

I do not remember all of the details of what was said. Mr. Sulya was apologetic and again explained about his wife's hysterectomy. I was asked if there was anything I wanted to say, and I shook my head no. Ed asked me if I would be OK staying in Mr. Sulya's class because no one else was teaching that course and I shook my head yes. Mr. Sulya left, and Ed asked me if I was OK. I nodded yes, but he knew I was not really OK, so he suggested we go for a walk.

We probably walked a couple of miles. It was a beautiful day, and it felt so good to be outside in the sunshine. We talked, but I do not remember the conversation. I do remember he was kind and compassionate, the way he was when he was reading books to the children sitting in his lap. At the end of the walk, he told me again how sorry he was that this had happened, and I felt grateful for his understanding. To my knowledge, the incident was never reported to anyone else or spoken of again. I went to class the next day, entering through the rear door of the classroom. Nothing was ever said, but I did not show up at the end of the day to clean the lab equipment. I got an A in the class.

CHAPTER 21

Father Charlie

I GREW UP in a Catholic family and now, half-jokingly, refer to my-self as a "recovering Catholic." God, religion, and everything associ-ated with it is very complicated for me. My religious experiences seemed to solidify an early belief that I was the problem in my family. My father always maintained a close relationship with the priest. He volunteered to change out the hymnals each month. He invited the priest over for dinner. He often went to the daily mass that only a few parishioners attended. I listened intently to the priest's homily, as my father assured me that if I listened and learned, I would figure out how to be more what God wanted me to be.

I remember hearing the Easter story and, while everyone was praising the resurrection of Christ, I was stuck on trying to understand how God had allowed his son to be tortured and believed it was nec-essary and good and that, somehow, the torture was for my benefit. I remember hearing people offer prayers for various people who were sick or dying and I wondered if God would not help me because I did not have anyone asking him to help me. My father had already made it clear to me that God did not want me to talk to him until I was fixed.

I remember my father taking me to see the priest and receiving a stern lecture on God's expectation to honor thy father and mother, after an incident where my father felt I had not been as quick to obey him as he felt I should have been. God, according to my father, was the reason he needed to teach me my lessons. I had been entrusted to him to raise, and he was not about to disappoint God by raising the horrible child I now was. However, when I was better and fixed, God's love would be amazing—he would take care of me and give me all that I needed in this world, as long as I lived my life the way he wanted.

I found all of these messages overwhelming and complicated, and to me, God was just a second father that I was constantly disappointing and who wished I had not been born. Nevertheless, I did find myself attracted to something about church—I loved the music. I liked learning the songs and then having something new to recite in my head when I was locked in the cold cellar. I liked watching all the people, and everyone seemed so happy in church. I was fascinated and intimidated by the priest and the power he had over the people in the church. I loved watching the people go up to receive the bread and wine.

Later, when I was in middle school and my father was no longer watching my every move, I often still chose to walk to church by myself. I think I was also attracted to the structure of the mass. I was good at memorizing, and I felt good when I knew exactly what to say when the priest said, "God be with you" and when to stand and sit and kneel. There were many rules, and I was getting very good at following rules.

Later, in my adult life, I decided I wanted to try to figure out the blanket of guilt I seemed to carry with me. My husband, Al, who had grown up in the Presbyterian Church, became interested in attending the Catholic Church, so we started attending on Sundays. Father Charlie was a tall, large man who seemed to command everyone's attention as soon as he walked into the church, and I think he would have done so even without the long robes and processional.

Al and I both liked Father Charlie. He followed the order of the mass, but he also incorporated a bit of humor now and then. He laughed at himself when he made mistakes. He seemed authentic and compassionate with everyone he met. After several months of attending Sunday mass and still struggling with the weight of guilt and no clear explanation for it, I decided to make an appointment with Fr. Charlie to talk about doing the traditional Catholic sacrament of confession.

Fr. Charlie made conversation with me easily, and I enjoyed our session. We did not actually do a "confession," because I could not clearly define the source of my guilt and was not very sure what to confess. I talked a little bit about my childhood and told him I had grown up in a "less than perfect" home. He invited me back to talk more about my religious journey and what might be creating the strong sense of guilt, as well as how to build a closer relationship with God. So, I began going to see Fr. Charlie on a weekly basis.

Not having done my therapy work yet, I did not notice as my interest in Fr. Charlie became stronger and my desire for him to approve of me became overwhelmingly important. I do not remember exactly how the conversation began one evening in our session, but it ultimately circled around to me wanting to be able to truly feel the love of God that so many people referenced. I expressed how, when I thought about God, I mostly just felt guilt.

I do not have an explanation for how we went from that to finding ourselves upstairs in his bed in the rectory. I vaguely recall a conversation about feeling closer to God through him and something else about proving my father was wrong and I deserved to be loved and treated like the beautiful woman I was. It may seem like the dots do not really connect from this conversation to us having sex, but for me it seemed like exactly the right progression. After all, I was just saying how I wanted to be loved, and now he was asking to love me. He was not mean or rough and he did not need to force me. I was a willing participant.

I left confused and sad, and my blanket of guilt just got heavier as I drove home and tried to process what had happened. I went back for one more session with Fr. Charlie, and we ended up in his bed a second time. After that, I started talking to my husband about moving and, within a few months, we left New York state. It was many years later when I finally confessed to my husband what had happened with Father Charlie, at which time I got to personally witness the amazing power of forgiveness from my husband.

I no longer attend the Catholic Church, and my understanding of God continues to be a source of confusion. Coming from a place of necessity, I simplify the issues for myself by believing that God is a source of positive, love energy in the world, and the more I can emulate that love with others, the closer I feel to the source of love myself.

PART II:
. . .YOU MUST SPEAK IN THE LIGHT!

"Do not be dismayed by the brokenness of the world. All things break. And all things can be mended. Not with time, as they say, but with intention. So go. Love intentionally, extravagantly, unconditionally. The broken world waits in darkness for the light that is you."

— L.R. Knost

"All the art of living lies in a fine mingling of letting go and holding on."

— Havelock Ellis

Foreword – Part II: The Healing Journey

MY STORY MAY be a difficult one to read. It is, in many ways, a difficult story to tell. I came from a childhood experience that was blatant with abuse. My father hated me. There is no gentler or simpler way to express that. He hated me. Although my memories go back to around four or five years of age, stories from my aunts, cousins, and siblings let me know that his hatred began from the moment of my birth.

He wanted a boy. He already had one girl and one boy, and he most definitely knew he preferred boys. He did have a second son after me, but the birth of another girl came as a serious disappointment. My father held some archaic beliefs about the differences between boys and girls. He believed boys represented strength and power. Ideas such as boys should not cry and boys should engage in "manly" tasks such as hunting and fishing were the norm in his thinking. Conversely, girls were viewed as weak and whiney. They should be in the background with as little presence and voice as possible.

My older sister had what some might describe as a tougher personality (or, as my father would describe it, one that made her more like a boy), and I happened to have a more sensitive personality. This was certainly a problem for my father. Therefore, I became the target. He was not a good parent to any of us, but the extreme physical, emotional, and sexual abuse were directed at me. He hated me.

Beyond his feelings toward me personally, my father was also an evil man. To me, he represents the epitome of the word. The dictionary defines someone who is *evil* as one who is profoundly immoral, wicked, malevolent, and depraved. It should also list my father as a synonym. His acts of evil were directed at anyone who challenged his ego in its very fragile form. They were also directed at the innocent who had done nothing but found themselves in the wrong place at the wrong time. His evil came through spontaneously as his mood would predict, or it would show itself in a planned and methodical attack on his latest victim.

My father directed his evil at me every hour of every day. It came in the form of unreasonable and extensive rules. It came in the form of broken bones, bruises, and stitches too numerous to count. It came through every derogatory and hurtful label that was imprinted on me even before I understood language. His evil was ever-present and was even manipulated through his absence. He used the tools of deprivation of food, light, touch, kindness, and basic humanity to change a young, unknowing child into a terrified, vulnerable being whose only defense was stillness and a false sense of being invisible.

I would not begin to walk the path to undo the damage of these experiences until many years later in life. Although I met some wonderful counselors through the years, the traditional schedule of once-a-week sessions mainly allowed me to manage issues that came up in my present-day life. I would not delve into the tangled web of my childhood until almost eighteen years later, at the age of thirty-nine, when I began psychoanalysis, a practice that continues at the time of this writing.

My analysis worked because my appointments were three, four, or five times a week. When I saw my therapist only once a week, there was too much time between appointments, time that enabled me to keep things hidden (even from myself), to keep walls strongly erected, and to keep defenses solidly in place without being aware they were even there. But when I saw my therapist every day or every other day, the feelings that I had buried so heavily under a cloak of protection began to seep through, and I began the real work of healing.

In one way, I've been very fortunate to have been able to compartmentalize my life into categories, and this skill enabled me to behave as though my childhood experience did not even happen, which allowed me to develop my roles in my career and as a wife and mother with what I thought was minimal residue from my upbringing.

But this compartmentalizing came at a significant price. In 2001, I was principal of an elementary school and I attended a crisis intervention training with other principals, counselors, and social workers in my district. I had been through many of these training sessions from my work as a counselor, prior to becoming a principal. The training was familiar, and I felt comfortable with the content I was learning.

At the end of the session, the presenter shared a video of families that had recently lost their homes to a series of wildfires in California. It was a moving video and I remember noticing a strong urge to cry that I had to fight to keep at bay while maintaining my professional role. For so many years, I had been trained how to not cry, and it struck me as odd that I suddenly had this internal urge to cry.

I was successful in pushing those emotions away, but over the next few days, I became aware of this heavy sadness I was carrying. My counselor training let me know that on some level I was connecting to a sense of loss and grief via the images in the video of these families who had lost everything. But I was confused because I had not experienced any recent loss in my life.

I pulled out the information from the training and found that the presenter worked at a nearby bereavement center, so I decided to give her a call and make an appointment. I met with her and explained what I was feeling ever since watching the video in her training session. She shared that she did not do counseling but could offer me a recommendation. She gave me the name of a local counselor and I went on my way.

I debated for days about whether to call the counselor, who was a man. The other times I'd tried counseling, I had worked only with women, with the exception of my first counseling experience with Fr. Charlie that had gone very badly. I had already learned in my life that I had a particular sensitivity to wanting the attention, love, and approval of men and had learned to stay away from them, like an alcoholic recognizing it's best not to hang around bars. So, I waited several weeks before calling the number. When I walked into my first appointment, I had no idea it would lead to the nineteen-plus-year journey I was about to embark on with this man.

CHAPTER 22

The Therapist

"At times, our own light goes out and is rekindled by a spark from another person. Each of us has cause to think with deep gratitude of those who have lighted the flame within us."

—Albert Schweitzer

THROUGHOUT MY LIFE, I have made several attempts at going for counseling, and the people I have worked with have always been helpful. I believe these people offered me what I needed at the time I was working with them. However, my healing really took hold when I began my psychoanalysis therapy with Ed.

As of this writing, we have now worked together for almost eighteen years, seeing each other anywhere from three to five times a week, depending on what we were working on at the time. To try to summarize that experience is almost impossible. The relationship has been my life-altering opportunity to understand myself differently and to learn, in an appropriate setting, how to establish and hold a healthy, intimate relationship, complete with feelings and boundaries.

There are times when I see Ed realistically, as the man he is, and other times when he is nothing less than a god in my life. There also have been times when he has become, in a safer way, the monster of my father. Transference is a necessary, powerful, frustrating, and healing part of the therapy process.

I will not try to tell anyone who has survived abuse what their path should look like. Analysis was the answer for me, but it may not be for someone else. I do advise others to keep searching for the resource(s) their gut tells them they need. I believe, deep inside, we all know and seek out what we need. Those engaging in that search should do so with an awareness that their judgment ultimately could be damaged by their previous experiences, so they should have a few options in place.

For example, it's important to find someone who has clearly defined boundaries. As people who have been abused, we have all had our boundaries mangled beyond recognition. What is an obvious breech of a boundary to most people may be acceptable to us because we have come to think it is what we deserve or it is the "norm." I discovered that my sense of my boundaries could not be trusted, and I am grateful every day that I ended up with a therapist who could hold the boundaries until I learned how helpful and necessary they are to the relationship.

One of my challenges was the deep hole left from wanting to be loved and cared for by my father and the rest of my family. I was willing to do anything to find someone to fill that hole (for example, Father Charlie and my high school chemistry teacher).

Quite honestly, if Ed had allowed it, this therapeutic relationship would have had a breakdown in boundaries as well. Those boundaries held firm entirely because of his strong ethical stance and not because I did not try to break them in every way. We had sessions where I was begging him to let me come and stay at his house for a weekend. I pleaded with him to have sex with me. It had nothing to do with sexual feelings and everything to do with the confused messages of using sex to feel valuable and wanted. For a long time, I was convinced that if he really cared about me, he would want to have sex with me (in a much nicer way than my father did). It took years for me to understand that it was because he cared about me that he would not have sex with me.

We had a great deal of work to do to keep the frame of therapy intact, and I will be eternally grateful for his wisdom in doing this, when I challenged it at every turn. A year or so into my time working with Ed in his home office, I went to his house when he was out of town and snooped around outside until I found a hidden key to his house. I used the key to go inside. I do not remember clearly all that I did when I was in his house, as I was in an altered state of thinking. I took pictures of the food in his refrigerator and his pantry. I looked at all the photographs of him and his family that I could find on the walls and in photo albums. I took pictures of every room in his house and of his cats sleeping on his bed. I crossed so many boundaries that day in my search for information.

As I share this, I still feel embarrassment and guilt. I also feel incredible gratitude that we survived such a breach of trust. At the next session, when I told Ed what I had done, he did not believe me at first, and I had to share where I found the key and show him the pictures of his pantry. He was understandably very upset.

The session itself is a blur as both of us were very emotional, but I clearly remember that even as upset as he was, he never raised his voice, he did not call me any names, and he did not become physical in any way. I got to witness anger and disappointment in their healthiest form. I was devasted and drowning in guilt. Part of me would have actually preferred him to become violent or scream and yell hurtful things as I knew what to expect with that. I did not know what to do with this more tempered and respectful response.

When I left at the end of the session, for the first time ever, we did not schedule a future session, as he needed some time to process how best to proceed. I waited as long as I could tolerate and then I began calling him. He responded to every call, but I could hear the distance between us and the formality of his responses. When I described how upset I was, he encouraged me to go the nearest hospital if my distress was not manageable. I begged him to forgive me. I pleaded for another appointment. Eventually, he asked me to meet with another analyst to review what had happened between us.

I met with a woman, another analyst, and explained all that had happened. She referred me to another male therapist whom I spoke with on the phone. However, after hearing the details of what had happened, he did not want to meet with me. Instead, he wanted to meet with my therapist. I contacted Ed and he agreed to meet with him. The two of them talked and Ed called and scheduled another session with me.

We talked a lot. I tried to explain what had happened that led me into his house and what I was seeking in the very limited way in which I understood it at that time. He talked about his session with the other therapist and we both knew it was going to have to be his decision whether to keep working with me or not. Ultimately, he moved through his emotions of anger and disappointment, and his dedication to quality therapy led him to the conclusion that we could continue our work together.

It would take years before we both truly understood the motivation behind my breaking into his house. A pivotal moment came for me a few months after the incident, when we were looking back again at what had happened. He commented that he thought perhaps in some way I was trying to demonstrate for him how violated I had felt as a child. He expressed tremendous empathy for me, as he said that his strong feeling of being violated must have been only a small piece of what I had experienced.

I remember immediately feeling confused. It was not until that moment that I thought that breaking into his house and going through his belongings would have caused him to feel "violated." Boundaries were so nonexistent for me that it honestly did not occur to me that I had violated Ed through my actions. It was not my intent to make him feel that way, as I had already developed many positive feelings for him, and the realization that I might have done something to cause him to experience any piece of what I'd felt as a child was difficult for me to accept.

This was my first and most valuable lesson in boundaries that are born out of a respect for another person. Boundaries are everything and when you are searching for the right therapist, find someone who will respect you and themselves enough to honor them. Find someone who can hold you in a safe space until you too can undo what happened to create your original sense of boundaries and learn what healthy boundaries really look like. Ed's consistency, loyalty, and insistence on the therapy structure provided the necessary safe environment I needed so I could access the horrors of my childhood.

After years of a strict therapy structure, the other gift Ed gave me was that of flexibility. Beyond the damage done to my emotional well-being, I had to work through issues of accepting and expressing my needs. Asking for, wanting, or needing anything in my house had been met with unspeakable punishments, so I learned not to have any needs.

Much to my surprise, I discovered years later that I have the same needs as everyone else, but these too had been mangled and twisted to be some awful representation of my badness. Needing to feel cared for, special, loved, and respected was, in my mind, equivalent to being a selfish, arrogant bitch who did not deserve the air she was breathing.

Learning to be OK with wanting to be loved was one of my biggest challenges. My first expression of this came almost ten years into my therapy, when I finally worked up the nerve to ask Ed if he would give me a hug. People who are involved with psychoanalysis learn quickly that no question is ever a simple one. The whole point of analysis is that everything gets studied and analyzed—words, behaviors, thoughts, feelings—all of it is up for careful and thorough examination. So, my request for a hug was not met with a yes or a no but instead with several sessions that ultimately exposed many feelings I held deep within about no one ever being allowed to touch me.

From my time as an infant, through the early years of my growing up, the message was that anyone who touched me would have dire consequences; so, no one ever kissed me goodnight, gave me a hug of support or a pat on the back, or held my hand when we walked. By verbalizing my request for a hug, I came face to face with the very human need to be touched and the deprivation I had experienced because that touch had been so blatantly refused.

Eventually, Ed granted my request and, over the years, when it was appropriate, I have freely requested and been granted more hugs. After that experience, I learned to ask for other things I might want or need, and every request was analyzed to determine the source of the need and what it might represent. Sometimes it was granted and sometimes it was not.

I have a great deal of respect for Ed and his judgment in navigating these challenging pieces. With the therapy framework so carefully held, he was able to slowly allow room to stretch an occasional boundary if he could determine a therapeutically healthy reason to do so.

One of my more challenging requests came in the form of asking him to give me a Christmas gift. Of course, I offered to give him the money he would spend on the present—what was important to me was for him to pick something out that would be a gift from him. As always, the request was followed with many hours of discussion, and ultimately, Christmas approached without receiving an answer to my request, as I was lost in the memories and emotions of being left out of holidays and presents that were never given or that were given and then taken away.

On December 23, I went in for my last appointment before the holiday, and the session began as usual. Then Ed, in a rare change in routine, indicated he needed to step out for just a minute. When he returned, he was holding a very large, wrapped box. This was not just a present—it was a giant present! The box was about three feet tall and I could hardly contain my excitement. I immediately burst into tears. After a few minutes of being overwhelmed with emotion, I opened the box to find a very large, brown, furry stuffed bear. This was not just any stuffed animal—it was the perfect stuffed animal because of how big and soft and cuddly it was.

Bear, as little Cheri in me immediately named him with the creativity and originality of a four-year-old, became an important part of my healing journey. I crawled into my warm, soft bed that night and pulled Bear close to me, and I fell asleep as the happiest girl in the world. Bear remains with me today. He has been a source of great comfort in some very challenging moments. He represents for me physical proof that the world can be a safe and secure space where one can feel loved and respected. There was a great deal of gift in that box!

Ed's continued balance between holding the boundaries tight while allowing the flexibility of meeting my many unmet needs through therapeutic strategies has allowed for many memories and feelings to surface and be processed. Some analysts might not agree with some of our more non-traditional experiences, but in every instance, the primary question was whether what I was asking would move me forward from a therapeutic perspective. I am eternally grateful for Ed's willingness to stretch himself in new ways as we explored how best to move my healing forward in a therapeutic manner.

One of the important methods of healing for me is to place a positive memory into the dark abyss in my mind that held a choice of only emptiness or extreme abuse. My father communicated a sense of me as nothing more than an insatiable and irritating bundle of needs. As a result, not only did I work desperately to squelch any need at all, I began to resent any needs that would surface. I hated myself for having the needs that are a part of being human. My ideas of myself are equivalent to a big sponge that can never be satisfied. Even once I began discovering and expressing my needs or wants, I did so with a sense of caution, as though, if I got too many of my needs met, I would surely become bothersome and irritating in demanding more and more.

Through some of the experiences Ed was willing to try, I began to discover that my needs actually could be met and, surprisingly, in a relatively simple way. Bear, for example, was an amazing Christmas gift and my fear was never realized that if I got one gift, I'd just keep wanting more and more—I never again felt the need to ask Ed for a Christmas gift. I also noticed that because I could now attach a positive experience around this Christmas gift, I was able to let go of the many horrible memories I had around that holiday. It was as though we discovered that once I had a positive experience to hold on to, the many negative ones lost their hold and power in my mind.

My childhood experience was filled with such deprivation and extreme abuse that there was very little and, in some cases, nothing at all, for me to build from. When Ed saw the positive effect the gift giving could have, he was willing to try other experiences as well. One time, we carved pumpkins in Ed's office; the memory of that day holds more space than the horrors I previously associated with Halloween. I experienced such pain from the many Thanksgivings when my father denied me any of the Thanksgiving food. This pain was lessened when Ed fixed an entire plate of leftovers, sharing with me what he had cooked for his family for that holiday.

The cravings I had as a little girl for someone to read to me have subsided, and they've been replaced with images of me sitting on Ed's floor with him reading and showing me the pictures from several books I'd selected. I spent part of one session with each of us coloring pictures in a Winnie the Pooh coloring book, where he graciously shared some tricks he had learned from his sisters on how to add shading for a positive artistic effect. Three years ago, one of my long-held dreams of living on the water came true when I bought a small, two-bedroom house on a private lake about an hour outside of where I was living. My husband and I had always dreamed of living on the water when we retired. Unfortunately, his unexpected death in 2010, after a very brief illness, prevented him from achieving that dream and left me not wanting to wait for it until retirement. Still, it was a difficult decision that required many hours of therapy as I took a huge leap of responding to something I really wanted without giving in to old feelings of being undeserving or selfish.

After getting settled in and feeling like this house was a clear representation of the peace I had been searching for my whole life, I expressed in one of my therapy sessions the desire to have Ed see my new home. Just as with all of my special requests, for months, we processed and analyzed what this meant, what it would do for me, and whether it would therapeutically move me forward.

Ultimately, I abandoned the request because I began having extreme nightmares of Ed drowning in my lake, being swallowed up by a sink hole just feet from my driveway, or other scenarios resulting in death or harm to Ed if he tried to visit.

We continued to work on this and many other issues before the idea resurfaced about a year later. This time, however, it finally happened. I had a therapy session in my home. We held the boundaries in place—this was not a social visit. I paid for his travel time and for the therapy time at my house. We processed the entire event, but mixed in to the typical analysis was an opportunity for me to share my home with a sense of pride and without a feeling that he would be harmed because I was "showing off."

My father had also communicated that anything I touched would be ruined or spoiled. In some instances, my looking at something would be enough to destroy it; my knowing about something would be enough to ruin it. He used this mantra to support his position to leave me out of everything. Sometimes, he had whispered conversations with everyone else in the house, with me sitting there not being allowed to hear a word of the plan. He threw food away if I touched it or looked at it.

This repeated behavior worked to deteriorate any sense of worth I had. Being forced to sit on the floor in the house or the car helped to cement my "place" in the family. My birthday each year was one of my father's worst days of the year. Obviously, my birth was a reminder of nothing good for him, so my birthday became a painful experience. His ritual of deciding if I should live another year on each birthday seemed genuine when I was a child, but as an adult I have come to see it as a sick, manipulative game.

After many years of therapy and healing, I approached my therapist with my biggest of all "wishes." Ed had a favorite possession, a 1968 Triumph TR6, and I wanted a ride in it, just around the block. So, I made the request for this as a birthday gift for my fifty-seventh birthday. It took me several sessions to make the request and of course several more sessions for us to analyze the desire. I shed many tears at the idea that my birthday was something to dread rather than celebrate and that for me to touch something important would destroy it.

We decided there would be therapeutic value in this experience, so he agreed. I had the usual nightmares the night before and arrived for my session on the designated day feeling tentative and suggesting that perhaps this was really not a good idea after all. Ed gently encouraged me so that I could have the experience and see that he and the car would be just fine, even after I rode in it.

The top was down, and he offered me a hat, but I declined, wanting to feel the wind in my hair. At first, I sat as still in the car as I had sat in my spot in the den in my family home fifty years earlier. I felt sure that if I stayed very still and hardly breathed, this would protect everything. Ed talked to me about the car and his experiences in it. I began to breathe a little more easily, and my body began to relax.

He did not take me around the block—he took me for miles. We went on some slow roads and some a little faster. We turned corners and stopped at stop signs. I felt the warm sun on my face and the wind blowing my hair. Having to sit on the floor of our family car meant that I had rarely been able to see where we were going, but that day, in the open air of the convertible, I saw and felt everything. I felt more alive on that birthday than I had on any of the fifty-six before it.

I could see in Ed's eyes that he wasn't worried at all about the effect my presence would have on his car. In fact, I could tell he was enjoying it too. We did not talk much during the ride, and yet volumes were spoken between us. He knew I was afraid. I knew he wouldn't do this if it were going to hurt either of us. He knew my birthdays had been awful, and I knew he wanted this one to be different. I knew the dark, cold, confined reality of the cold cellar, and he knew that a ride on a warm, sunny day in an open convertible would go a long way to moving terrifying memories out and replacing them with fun and happy memories. We had been on this journey together for almost eighteen years, and this thirty-minute birthday ride in his most special car was literally and metaphorically as far from where our journey had begun than either of us could have imagined. I wish for others who've lived through abuse the opportunity to heal their deepest wounds with someone as intelligent, skilled, loyal, steadfast, compassionate, humorous, dedicated, creative, flexible, and caring as I have had. Everyone deserves it and as I have finally come to understand, that includes me!

CHAPTER 23

Sadness and Grief

"She was no longer wrestling with her grief, but could sit down with it as a lasting companion and make it a sharer in her thoughts."

—George Eliot

WHEN I STARTED my therapy at age thirty-nine, I had rarely cried in my lifetime. My father's lessons on not crying were so etched in my being that tears simply would not flow. I felt sadness, but crying just didn't happen. I tried to hide that when my older brother, Steve, died at thirty-six years old. And at the time of my three miscarriages. And through my mother's funeral. I was embarrassed, knowing that the normal response to grief is to cry, and yet for me, the tears just would not come.

In my first session of therapy, I explained to Ed that I was there because I had an overwhelming sense of sadness and felt as though I was living with a huge, empty hole in my heart. But even as I described those feelings, I did so with a sense of detachment. It would not be until after about ten months of therapy, four to five times per week, that the first tears started falling from my eyes. And when they did, I immediately wiped them away before they could make it from my eye to my cheek. This wiping of tears would become a point of discussion for many, many years to come, as Ed encouraged me to just "let the tears flow." However, in a motion as natural to me as breathing, I would quickly wipe away any "evidence" of crying as though I might still be severely punished if it was discovered that I had cried.

Memories of my father pulling me from the cold cellar, into the light of the basement, shining a flashlight into my eyes to determine if I had in fact been crying, came to me the moment a tear began to form all these years later, sitting in Ed's office. There were times when Ed expressed a genuine concern that I would hurt myself from rubbing away my tears so intensely. So, when my second brother, Paul, died at the age of forty-two, and my husband died a couple of years after that, the tears I cried in those days held the grief of their deaths and so many other losses before them.

I have learned that grief in one moment becomes a part of every future grieving, and that both resolved and unresolved grief will eventually show themselves at a time that is most unexpected—a news story on the television, a touching moment in a movie, a neighbor relaying a sad story about someone I'd never met. Even a Hallmark commercial could suddenly cause the tears to well up and sadness flow out. Getting in touch with my sadness was the first time I experienced emotion in a genuine and authentic way in my therapy. And while it took months for it to begin, and years before it felt comfortable, it is now an emotion I experience easily and frequently in my therapy, because there was and is much to feel sad about.

As an adult, I have had many opportunities to experience grief. When I was thirty-three years old, I was awakened at four o'clock in the morning with a phone call from my sister, informing me that my brother Steve had died earlier in the evening, probably from a heart attack. I had just spoken with my brother two weeks earlier, on his thirty-sixth birthday. In the days following his death, I thought back several times to my call to wish him a happy birthday. He told me about his enjoyable day with his twelve-year-old daughter, Jesse, and his ten-year-old son, David, and shared with pride the details of his game of pool with David. I replayed our last conversation many times in my head and felt good that we had at least had that time to chat, not knowing he would be dead just a couple of weeks later. About a month after his death, I went to my mailbox and got my mail. In it was my telephone bill, which detailed all my long-distance calls. I looked at my brother's number on February 11th and again remembered the birthday call. But then, I looked at the total time of the call and saw that it was two minutes and forty seconds. In my mind we had talked at least for half an hour, and now I found out it was not even three minutes. I immediately felt the wave of grief that sometimes comes with the force of a tsunami. But at that time, I didn't have access to my tears and the grief got pushed away, to be uncovered later when my younger brother, Paul, also died of a heart attack at age forty-two.

After I had been in therapy for about eight years and had cried tears of grief for both of my brothers, I had a whole new experience with grief. It was the day before Thanksgiving and my husband, Al, had a ten o'clock appointment with our family doctor. He had gone to the doctor two weeks earlier with an annoying cough from a cold, but the cough just wasn't going away. At some point during the appointment, Al inadvertently pocket dialed me on his cell phone. In spite of my screaming from my end of the phone, he didn't hear me or notice that we had a phone connection. Then I heard the doctor walk into the room. I probably should have hung up the phone on my end, but I didn't. I heard the doctor tell him that they'd noticed a shadow on his chest X-ray, and they wanted to send him for a more detailed picture of his lungs. At two o'clock, he called me from work and mentioned that he had gone to a second doctor. I confessed that I already knew because of the pocket dial. He told me that the doctor had called and asked him to come back in at four o'clock and to "bring a family member." We both knew that meant there was going to be bad news.

At four, we arrived at the doctor's office and everyone was anxiously waiting to finish with the last patients so they could begin their Thanksgiving holiday. The atmosphere was light, and people's jovial moods felt confusing as we walked into the office, knowing we were going to hear something bad. The doctor proceeded to inform us that while additional testing would be necessary, it looked very much like Al had stage 4 lung cancer. We had many questions and, while they tried to be as helpful as possible, the answers were vague and the doctor simply summed it up by saying, "This is a very bad diagnosis and we're very sorry." The doctor walked out of the office and Al and I just looked at each other and we both began to cry.

We cried more tears when we shared the news with our son, Ian. He was eighteen and home from college for the Thanksgiving holiday. We all tried to be optimistic and discussed all kinds of options for treatments we really knew nothing about. We unanimously decided that whatever happened, cancer was treatable, and we would get through the treatments. We would see a specialist on Monday after the holiday and figure out next steps. So, Ian went back to college on Sunday and prepared for his first semester of college finals, while Al and I trekked off to numerous doctors, all day Monday.

On Tuesday, we went back to get test results and prepare for our plan of action. We were informed that Al's brain scan had already detected fourteen tumors in his brain, and the doctor was shocked that Al was still alive. He would have to start radiation immediately to secure any additional time. The prognosis was not good. With radiation and chemotherapy treatments, Al might be with us for twelve to eighteen months. We were able to keep him at home, and Ian chose to not go back to college after the winter break as he wanted as much time with his dad as possible. On February 8th, with Ian and me lying in the bed next to him, Al left this earth just ten weeks after his diagnosis and three months shy of our twenty-fifth wedding anniversary. My work in therapy allowed me to shed many, many tears for Al, for Ian, for myself, and for the natural grief that occurs when you lose someone you love.

As with everything else, my father was wrong about sadness and tears. They are not a sign of weakness; they are evidence of humanness. They are witnesses to a compassionate heart. Every animal that was tortured and killed was deserving of oceans of tears. Someone who could hear the wail of a cat being injured or hold a dying puppy in their hands and not feel sadness is not me and is not someone I would want to be. When I allow my tears to flow now, I honor them. I know they are a much better representation of who I am as a person and who I feel good about being as a person.

I had occasional contact with my father once I moved away from Maine. My sense of guilt and obligation kept nagging at me to try to be a good daughter. My older sister hated my father and would have no contact with him. My older brother, Steve, lived in the same town and would see him on occasion, and my younger brother, Paul, lived a couple of hours away and would also see him a few times a year. After Steve's death, at his funeral, all of us watched my father and something shifted for us.

Contact at that point became very rare. My father's second wife occasionally called me to update me on my father's status. He was living in a rehabilitation hospital and had one of the longest documented cases of Alzheimer's disease in the state of Maine. I went to see him at the nursing home, and he didn't know who I was or even that I was there. I had a polite visit with his nurse, who commented on what a wonderful man he was and how much everyone there loved him. I looked at him in his wheelchair and thought about all the years I had spent processing my memories and how he had now lived about twenty years of his life not being able to remember anything. He died a few years ago. I did not go to the funeral. I did not cry any tears—not because I was holding them back, but because I felt no sadness for his dying.

My father's idea of toughness was not really about being tough. It was about learning to be cold and heartless, and I'm glad that I never really learned that lesson. I stopped my tears in his presence as an act of self-preservation, but I held those tears deep inside me and eventually let them flow, knowing that the horrific experiences that created them warranted every last drop. I never became the person he wanted me to be—someone who did not feel the pain or sadness—only a person who could hide it inside.

Coming to that realization later in life eventually allowed me to learn to like and respect myself. Our world still tells people, usually men, that tears and crying are to be controlled and hidden. That message is not only damaging but totally wrong for a healthy emotional life. Our tears are often an indication that we are in touch with the pain and sadness that happens in this world, and to hide that denies an important part of who we are as a human race.

"There is a sacredness in tears. They are not the mark of weakness, but of power. They speak more eloquently than ten thousand tongues. They are the messengers of overwhelming grief, of deep contrition, and of unspeakable love."
—Washington Irving

CHAPTER 24

Dancing with Anger

"Do not teach your children never to be angry; teach them how to be angry."

—Lyman Abbott

OVER MY MANY years of therapy, I eventually began to reconnect with the emotional part of my life. It happened slowly and in stages, but I began to recognize, understand, and learn to tolerate sadness, grief, joy, loneliness, fear, guilt, and many of the other normal parts of the wonderful experience of being human.

Anger, however, seemed to be in a category all to itself and was by far my greatest challenge to identify, feel, and accept. I was aware that I never seemed to feel angry, but for much of my life, I wore that with a sense of pride. Somehow, that made me a better person, to be able to tolerate injustices and remain calm and unscathed. Understanding the denial of the feeling and the damage being done by such denial came only after I had been in therapy for many years.

As I began to become curious about where my anger was, I started looking for outlets to help me get in touch with it. I attended several amazing workshops known as "externalization" experiences. Elizabeth Kübler-Ross had developed these workshops through her work with people in their final stages of life, to help them, and later all people, find a safe and healthy approach to working through unresolved emotions—especially anger. I met some amazing people at these workshops and witnessed incredible pain paired with phenomenal strength.

However, I continued to struggle to find and express anger. I eventually understood that the anger was in there, and I was expressing it but not as anger. It was misdirected and showed itself as guilt, as hatred toward myself, as deep darkness and depression—anything but actual anger. My mantra, when asked if I was angry with my father for all that he did to me, was to say I really did not want to give him any more time or energy. Once again, I wore as a veil of pride that I could "turn the other cheek" after all these experiences. I latched on to public voices that said being angry kept you stuck in your past and, to free your own life for peace and happiness, you only had to let go of anger and learn to forgive. I surrounded myself with quotes to support my position:

"Anger is often more hurtful than the injury that caused it."
—English
"Anger is one letter short of danger."
—Eleanor Roosevelt
"The anger of the prudent never shows."
—Burmese
"Anger is a wind, which blows out the lamp of the mind."
—Robert Green Ingersoll
"Anger dwells only in the bosom of fools."
—Albert Einstein
"Whatever is begun in anger ends in shame."
—Benjamin Franklin
"Anger makes you smaller, while forgiveness forces you to grow beyond what you are."
—Cherie Carter-Scott

So, I kept my anger away and I forgave my father. I actually had forgiven him many, many years before. The problem was that I'd forgiven him without ever actually holding him accountable—I'd skipped that part. I went from blaming myself for everything to proclaiming ownership of my future by not needing to be angry about what had happened and graciously forgiving. But I discovered I was very wrong.

As often happened in my therapy, the first hints of my anger came out with Ed. It seemed to start around issues of feeling left out. Why could he not share more information with me about himself? What harm was there in my knowing what he did over the weekend or if his daughter was engaged or what the rest of his house looked like? I wanted in. I wanted to be a part of his family. I vaguely remember even suggesting he did not have to include me in his family activities. I could just sit quietly in the living room and observe him and his family.

In the beginning, if I felt even a hint of being irritated with Ed, I would cancel my session. I would give myself a few days to think about it and bring myself to a clearer understanding, which was actually code for giving me time to bury the seeds of anger so that it was no longer a possibility. I did not do this on a conscious level, and it took a long time before I even recognized that pattern.

A moment of marked progress came when I showed up for my therapy appointment and there was a different car in the driveway. Of course, if any little thing was different, I immediately had to check in about it, so I started the session by asking whose car was in the driveway. Ed explained that he had gotten a new car. In a normal situation, the appropriate response might be "congratulations!", but I got very quiet and we both knew I was pulling away. And because it had happened so many times before, we knew I had just stepped on another mine in the minefield I live in. I could feel an energy growing inside me, and heat seemed to be emanating from my stomach. My breathing began to change and, in that moment, I finally recognized that I was angry. I wanted to run. I think I might have even suggested that I needed to leave and would be back tomorrow. However, my gifted and patient therapist helped me to stay with the feeling. Eventually I was even able to tell him that I was angry that he had not shared with me earlier that he had gotten a new car. Because I now lived farther away, some of our sessions were being done via Skype, and we'd had several Skype sessions since he bought the car.

After all this time, he knew I struggled with changes, and yet he did not choose to forewarn me during one of the Skype sessions that I would see a new car in the driveway when I arrived for an in-person session. Furthermore, why would this be something he would deliberately keep from me? That was a challenging session as I struggled to be accepting of my anger and manage my fear of rejection if I expressed it to him and my worry that my anger would incite him to be angry with me.

Anger terrified me, as one would expect after what I had experienced. My model for being angry was an out-of-control, raging psychopath. At a minimum, anger meant I was a disappointment and should feel only guilt. At its worst, anger meant pain, terror, torture, death, and solitude. I had chosen to keep anger away for a very long time—so far away that I was not even "burying" it, because for many, many years I never gave it enough space to even know I had something to bury. It just did not exist within me.

As I began to understand how anger can give us a voice when we need to speak up to stop something bad from happening, and how anger can give us energy to take actions when they are needed, I wanted mine back. Wherever it was, I wanted to find it and learn how to use it in a strong, healthy way to protect me and serve me the way it did for others. Part of what made anger so confusing was that I was able to access this assertiveness in two arenas in my life: for my son and in my work life. If I needed a voice in those situations, it came to me easily and effectively. I did not become a raging monster. I was appropriately respectful with my anger when it arose in those environments, so I knew I had the skills, but when it came to my history and my therapy life it was deep in hiding.

I have met some people with the opposite struggle, where anger is their primary emotion and they have to work to not be angry all the time. I feel fortunate that anger did not take its hold on me in that way, but I still wanted access to it. We tried a variety of strategies. In addition to the workshops I attended, I read books. I tried writing journal entries and writing letters. We attempted role-playing activities. I bought a punching bag. I pounded on thick phone books with rubber hoses. I twisted and pulled on towels. I was determined to access my anger, but of all the work I did, it was honestly one of the slowest and most difficult challenges I was to face.

At the time of this writing, it remains an issue I have not yet mastered. We have made progress, and I am hopeful for the continued work, but I know this is an area that will still require focus as I continue to seek to have access to my anger in a healthy and appropriate way. I used to be terrified that if and when I found the anger, it would come out in me similarly to how it came out in my father. After all, I am biologically made from his genes. However, I no longer worry about that.

In the moments when I am aware that I'm angry, I've noticed that my anger does not change who I am as a person, and the person I am never, ever wants to hurt anyone or anything. This is a marked difference between my father and me, and recognizing that has allowed me to feel safe in letting the seeds of appropriate anger begin to grow.

Ed's new car and his decision not to share about it in advance gave way to many hours of processing several healing threads. First, I began to access more of the feelings related to being locked in the cold cellar and left out of all family information. I got in touch with what it felt like to have family members whisper information because my father's orders were to keep things from me.

It was a common understanding that if I knew a piece of information, it would spoil the event. Similarly, if I happened to glance in the fridge and see what was there, my father would immediately throw the food in the garbage. He would take away presents that were given to my siblings if they showed them to me or shared them with me in any way. Leaving me out was a deliberate and calculated strategy my father used to keep me disconnected from everyone. This left me not only feeling excluded but carrying a sense that I was not good enough to have information shared with me, and in fact, my mere knowing would cause harm and pain. When Ed chose not to share the news of his new car, all of this came flooding back.

Additionally, because Ed knew my sensitivity to changes, I felt his not letting me know in advance was a set-up. I felt as though he deliberately did not tell me so I could practice managing my reactions to change. This thinking uncovered the many feelings of manipulation and frustration I experienced around all of my father's lessons.

Until I experienced this misconception about Ed's motives, I had not realized how many feelings I really had about my father's daily lessons. It took several sessions for me to access the anger I felt with my father for repeatedly setting me up in no-win situations in the interest of making me good enough.

Finally, if Ed really knew me and cared about me, why would he not do everything in his power to help me avoid stepping on another mine by simply sharing the car news in advance? This third reaction helped me access the feelings of a little girl who wanted to be protected by her father. Isn't a father supposed to want to make the path easier for his child? Doesn't a father want to help the child feel good rather than frightened or sad?

Ed's decision to not protect me from the discovery of the new car reminded me how much I wished I'd had a daddy who protected me and wanted me to feel happy and ultimately how angry I felt that I didn't. As much as I would never have admitted it for several weeks after showing up for the now infamous "new car" session, I did come to understood that Ed's wisdom in this situation allowed several unresolved issues to surface, including my first healthy processing of angry feelings.

Over time, I would have several more experiences with being angry with Ed, as naturally happens in relationships. It did not happen instantly, but over time, I slowly began to identify angry feelings and learned to let them be seen and heard. It is not yet as spontaneous as I would like it to be, but I am making progress!

CHAPTER 25

Guilt/Shame

"There are two kinds of guilt: the kind that drowns you until you're useless, and the kind that fires your soul to purpose."

—Sabaa Tahir

"Shame should be reserved for the things we choose to do, not the circumstances that life puts on us."

—Ann Patchett

WHILE MANY OF my emotions were buried deep, the one I have defaulted to in all situations is that of guilt or shame. It took a very long time for me to begin to separate these strong feelings, but I have now come to understand them and see guilt as different from shame. Guilt is related to behaviors or acts. I was drowning in guilt for many of the behaviors in which I participated. When people are repeatedly forced to engage in behaviors that are reprehensible to their conscience, they eventually forget the part of the scenario that was about being forced.

In my situation, I simply began to see myself as this horrible person who had engaged in these horrible behaviors. Because I can "watch" myself (as memories in my mind) do such horrific things to animals or be part of behaviors that hurt other people, I can see myself only as bad and totally responsible. Also, by holding myself responsible for these behaviors instead of my father, I protected myself from a rage that was not safe to direct toward him and perhaps, in some small way, also allowed me to think I had some control over a situation that was totally out of my control.

Shame, I have to come to understand, is related not necessarily to specific behaviors or acts, but rather to who a person is believed to be. Eventually my guilt for engaging in cruel behaviors with my pets became an embedded shame, as I began to see myself as someone who was simply a bad person from the inside out.

It would take many years of analyzing and reliving specific incidents to begin to separate my forced participation from my father's intentional cruelty. It took even longer to begin to let go of my sense that badness emanated from my very core and that I was simply "bad" from the moment of my birth. In an effort to avoid spoiling me or giving me too much attention, my father did not allow me to be picked up from my crib when it was feeding time. Instead he made a wooden contraption that held my bottle for me in the crib, and my mother could adjust the height as the bottle drained. I was obviously too little to have memories of this and learned of it as an adult from an aunt who my father scolded for wanting to hold me with my bottle when she visited. However, even without the direct memories, I believe the sense of not being worthy of being held or touched was probably what planted the seedlings of my long-held beliefs that I was bad from my very core.

My father was intentional in how he manipulated the circumstances of all events around my behavior. No matter what had happened, it was my responsibility and mine alone. The dichotomy of having control over nothing and being responsible for everything was a complicated mess that took many years to unravel. Even now, I have to take a step back and ask myself if the situation at hand really is my responsibility to either feel guilty about or fix.

Much of my focus on responsibility is related to being accountable for every one of my father's feelings and experiences. My very patient therapist helped me to understand this and resolve it through years of me trying to read his mind and anticipate his every reaction and feeling. In addition, helping me understand that it is impossible for a person to do this with another person, he also wanted me not to be burdened with a responsibility that is not mine. A minor example: when scheduling sessions, usually the patient and/or the therapist will offer their availability and they agree on times that work for both of them. For many, many years, my primary concern in scheduling was to find times that would be most convenient for Ed. I would work to ensure that it would not to be too early or too late in the day. I would try to avoid Friday afternoons because, I thought, everyone likes to be done early on Fridays, right? I would try to learn his schedule for other regular appointments so he could go from one to another and not have a gap he needed to fill in his day. None of these criteria came from him. It was all about me trying to anticipate his every need and feeling. I had little awareness of the craziness I was creating with my own schedule to make it happen. I would like to say, after almost twenty years, this is issue is resolved, but that would not be truthful. My awareness has grown, and I have learned to find a better balance between my needs and someone else's, but it is not a natural behavior and may always be one I have to pay attention to in my relationships.

At one point in my therapy, when we were working on my sense of guilt and shame, we began discussing how bad I felt that my father had to have a daughter that he hated so much. I talked about the unbelievable depth of love and pride I feel for my son and how I could not imagine how horrible it must have been for my father to have to look at me every day and feel such disappointment and hatred. I began to cry and shared with Ed how guilty I felt.

I told the story of one night when my father left me one of his handguns to put under my pillow, with a plea to shoot myself to put him and the world out of their misery before he had to face another day with me as his daughter. As I cried and tried to describe my guilt, I just kept talking about how hard it was to see his look of disappointment the next morning when he came in and found me still alive. I described how he would talk about how unbelievably sad he was that

I had not used the gun and how awful it would be for him to go on.

In a very important moment when the puzzle pieces shift a bit and fall into place, Ed asked me "Why would he be acting so disappointed when he saw you?"

I did not understand why this was a confusing idea and reiterated my father's anguish at finding me still alive.

Ed said, "I know what he was telling you, but why would he be surprised you were alive? If you had shot yourself, he would have heard the gunshot during the night. There should not have been any element of surprise when he entered your room in the morning."

It was my first moment of realization that perhaps what my father did was an intentional manipulation and not a true picture of a man in distress over having such a terrible daughter. As a little girl, I couldn't see beyond the apparent drama and distress and avoid absorbing it as part of the weight of guilt and responsibility, but now as an adult, Ed's logical question began to open the door to a new perspective. My father would have to have known I was still alive, which meant he must have been acting in the scene that played out. It would be many years still until these ideas began to be real and take hold, but every piece of my healing had to begin in a moment, and in that moment, I had the first idea that perhaps my father's interpretation of me as "bad" was not actually reality but part of a complicated, manipulative madness he created to keep me settled into the terror and abuse.

Guilt and shame in an abuse situation are deeply entangled in the confusion over responsibility. Many years later, when I served as a crisis volunteer at our local domestic violence and sexual assault center, it was a thread I would see repeatedly, in almost every call. It is a part of the power the abuser uses to keep the survivor confused and beholden to him or her. It is complicated and challenging to correct.

I have had to learn to use other healthy scenarios in my life as a guide to determine levels of responsibility. It is a much clearer picture for me with other people, so I take myself out of the scenario and ask, "Would I say that my son is responsible if this happened to him?" or "Would I hold a colleague responsible for that person's actions?" This allows me to evaluate current situations without the confusion of my history influencing whether the outcome is truly my responsibility or not.

I still can get caught, as guilt is my "go to" default response, but it is far more manageable and no longer nearly as disruptive to my life. I also have used my strong sense of guilt and responsibility as an important clarification to help me understand how I am different from my father. The mere fact that I experienced such a high degree of guilt for every act I was made to do and my father seemed to never experience guilt or responsibility helps to remind me that, given a choice, I would never have participated in those behaviors and, therefore, they are not who I am as a person.

CHAPTER 26

The Many Parts of Me

"Our life together has just begun. You are the best part of me my little one!"

—Author unknown

ONE OF THE most embarrassing and shameful parts of the effects of my childhood is the work I have had to do with dissociation. Dissociation is a process by which our minds separate us from the present moment. All of us experience dissociation every day. When you find you've driven several miles in the car and can't really recall the last few streets you passed or the red light you stopped at because your mind was preoccupied with other thoughts, you experienced dissociation in its mildest form.

At the other extreme, most of us have seen movies with people who have what was once known as "split personality disorder" and shared in the fascination as we watched the character go from a functioning adult male to an angry teenage boy or a psychotic, out-of-control woman, and so on.

To be accurate about my journey requires me to talk about my issues with dissociating. The reason this is challenging to talk about is that in my work life as a teacher, principal, trainer, and educator, as well as in my roles as wife, mother, friend, and neighbor, I have always wanted to be seen as healthy and "normal." When a person starts talking about dissociating, red flags go up and people conjure images based on their limited experiences from movies and television, and suddenly the concept of "normal" moves toward the spectrum of "crazy."

So, for the record, dissociating does not mean crazy and it rarely looks like what we see portrayed on television. However, our minds are beautiful things that protect us when we need it the most, and for many people who have experienced trauma, there is often a level of dissociation that has helped us to survive. I am no exception to that. I do not break out into other personality types, but in the many hours and days in the cold cellar, I did discover parts of myself that could take on some of the feelings and experiences my little brain and body could not manage alone. So, let me introduce the parts of me that helped me to survive the indescribable day-to-day life I had to endure.

In my lessons on how to experience pain without crying, I learned how to dissociate from pain. As an adult, that means that I have been able to have all my dental work (root canals, crowns, fillings, etc.) done without any Novocain or other numbing drugs. It means that when I was in college and was a passenger in a car accident in which my left arm was broken, I was able to get out of the car, walk up to the EMT, and say, "I need an X-ray because my arm is broken," without any feeling of discomfort.

On the surface, it might appear in these situations that the ability to dissociate from feelings of pain is a positive trait and, believe me, I would often wear it with pride. However, I came to understand that being that disconnected from my body when it was in pain meant I was also not in touch with my body when it was tired, hungry, satisfied, sick, stressed, and the whole array of other feelings we all experience as a part of living. As I have learned to be more in touch with my emotions through my therapy, I have been less able to dissociate with painful experiences and, at the time of this writing, I am booked for a dental appointment in a few weeks and plan on asking for Novocain because tolerating pain is something I no longer want to ask my body to endure.

I needed help with the numerous rules I had to remember. My brain simply could not keep track of them all. The part of me that mastered this skill, which I named Dora, was vital to our survival. I cannot explain exactly how it happened, but each time a new rule was introduced I was able to give it to Dora, and she would carry the burden and stress of remembering it. And she did a phenomenal job. As I have done my work in therapy, I have come to understand that the dissociating did not create separate people but just compartmentalized parts of myself that I used to reduce my need to be present for all of the horrible experiences. Therapy meant inviting those parts to come back together, much like the puzzle pieces of the heart I described in my introduction. Dora no longer exists as a separate person within me, but instead I see those qualities she represented for me as a child as a part of who I am. As an adult, our memory and organizational skills have been a strength in my work life. As a child, those skills allowed me to manage far more information than a little girl should ever have to organize.

The sexual abuse by my father (and his friends) was so terrifying and overwhelming that I created Susan to carry that burden. Susan was able to behave in the adult ways my father sought, while protecting me as a little girl from enduring these acts that are painful and unnatural for young children. When you hear people describe a traumatic experience, they will often say, "It was as though I was watching it on a movie screen" or "It was like I was on the ceiling, just watching from above."

These are additional examples of how dissociation can be used to help us survive trauma. Susan served in that capacity for me whenever the situation became a sexual experience. Once again, while her serving that role was lifesaving for me as a child, it was problematic as an adult when I was unable to be present for healthy, adult sexual experiences.

It may be different for others who have survived trauma, but for me, dissociation was not a planned experience. So, Susan stepped in with Mr. Sulya. Susan was there for Fr. Charlie. I needed to do a great deal of work to be present in my healthy adult experiences. While Susan is no longer a presence for me, and I feel she has been integrated with me, I suspect that if I were to have the horrible experience again of being raped, I would find that she is still within me somewhere, ready to once again help me survive.

Oftentimes in counseling or therapy situations, people will talk about being in touch with their "inner child," referring to the younger part of themselves. It could be a younger part that needed healing or the younger part that helps them experience fun and joy in a childlike manner.

My "inner child," Cheri, has taken the longest to integrate and not feel like a totally separate part of me. For most of my life, Cheri has been the little girl that experienced everything. In some ways, I felt as though I brought Cheri along with me when I left Maine and started my new life. When I married my husband and moved to Florida, I started having people call me Cheryl, the name on my birth certificate but rarely used growing up.

Cheri was with me, but it was as though she lived in a small space inside of me, protected from everything. She was warm and well fed, but I pretty much just left her alone.

I did not want any more bad things to happen to Cheri, but I soon discovered that I carried with me many of the negative feelings my father had for her. Ultimately, I blamed her for everything that happened. I was not nearly as cruel as my father, but underneath, I did believe that Cheri was needy and selfish. I saw her as weak and as a problem to the world. Everything he felt for me I put onto Cheri and tucked it away so that Cheryl could function as a successful wife, mother, teacher, principal, friend, and so on. The bulk of my twenty years of therapy has been about learning to see Cheri through my own eyes and not my father's and to love Cheri as my inner child and not someone I had to be ashamed of and keep hidden.

When I was a little girl, my father used to take me to the grocery store and point out to me the little girls he saw that he wished could be his daughters instead of me. I used to study all those little girls to try and learn what they had that I didn't have. I used to watch their movement so that I might be able to behave in the exact same way they did. If we walked close enough, I would listen for every word they would say so that I could repeat those words and try to make myself just like the little girls my father wanted, so he would want me too.

Over time, this created a sense of not being able to tolerate myself and desperately wanting to be anyone but who I was. I think that creating a separate Cheri to be the little girl he could not stand was actually a very clever way for my mind to protect me, because if I could not separate out this horrible child from myself, I would have to die.

Sometimes when I think about the number of years I went to therapy, four to five times per week, I feel embarrassed at how long it has taken to sort all this out. But then when I remember the trips through the grocery store and how my father conveyed those deliberate and debilitating messages over and over, I become more forgiving of Cheri and of Cheryl for how long it takes to undo the incredible damage that was a part of our daily life.

In my first year of therapy, almost twenty years ago, two specific memories paint a picture of where I started. The first was when I accidently knocked over my water bottle while sitting in Ed's office. A little bit of water spilled before I could grab the bottle and pick it up. Within thirty seconds I was curled up in the corner of Ed's office, and it took a great deal of work to bring me back to the present day.

The second memory, from a few months later, was when I ran into Ed in the grocery store. He said hello and from his perspective, everything would have been fine. But I had to walk out and leave my cart behind and get to my car, as I realized I had just literally stood there and peed my pants on the grocery store floor. I shared with him my experience in my next therapy session and was relieved that he had not noticed.

Transference (moving the feelings and experiences of the past onto another person, in this case Ed) was an essential part of unlocking the many feelings buried deep inside of me. The two experiences of spill-ing the water and the grocery store meeting gave both Ed and me a glimpse of the terror of my childhood that we would spend the next nineteen plus years sorting out. When I think about that, I am grate-ful for my mind protecting me in whatever ways it needed to so that I could survive. I eventually began to see Cheri differently, and I now credit her loving heart as the part that saved us.

CHAPTER 27

My Relationship with Food

"There are people in the world so hungry that God cannot appear to them except in the form of bread."
—Mahatma Gandhi

MANAGING WEIGHT AND food is a challenge for many people, even if they have no history of abuse or neglect. Food is a source of pleasure and plays a vital part in many aspects of our lives. We use it in a social manner when we gather at a table with family or friends or get together to go out to eat. The measure of a good party or event is often the quality and variety of food options. We use it to help us feel good at the end of a stressful day and to celebrate major events in our lives.

So, my battle with managing food and weight throughout my life has had many of the present-day challenges most of us face. However, if we add to the picture the way my father used and abused food in my childhood, the challenges I face today have been a true lifelong battle. When I was a young child, my father kept food from me most of the time. When I was not in the cold cellar, I often ate my dinner under the table, scrambling for scraps dropped on the floor, competing with an also hungry dog or cat.

When I was in the cold cellar, food became a strong focus, bordering on obsession. As my father left me with only a small amount of food and water, and I had no sense of how long I would need them to last, it became a minute by minute internal battle on whether to respond to my aching craving for a bite of food or listen to my brain telling me to hold out as long as possible because waiting another hour could be the difference between surviving or not.

Given that I never did actually starve to death, I have often been upset with myself for having had such a strong reaction and spending so much time obsessing over measuring out the food. I once told Ed, "Obviously, he was timing it in such a way that he was not going to let me starve to death, so why didn't I trust that?" But I know now that as a small girl I could never have reached that conclusion, and every time I heard the cold cellar door close, I would begin the negotiating process between my brain and my stomach. Added to that was the responsibility I felt when he would lock me up with a kitten or rabbit or mouse and I knew they were hungry too—food became a powerful force in my life.

Even when I became homeless, my resources were so limited that I was nervous about spending money on food and found myself scrounging again for scraps. I carried the power food had over me as a child into my adult life. I found it challenging to put restrictions on myself, even when those limitations would actually help me. It was as though I was walking around thinking, "No one is going to tell me what I can and can't eat ever again." Unfortunately, that included me!

My father often used food as a punishment, when he would force me to eat a disgusting item or a food product doused in hot sauce. If I showed any signs of being hungry and needing food, it was not unusual for him to force me to eat an unreasonable quantity of food until I vomited and then force me to eat the vomit. It seemed I was constantly in a battle between deprivation of food, craving it so much it hurt, and food being used against me to hurt me so much that I wanted nothing to do with it.

As an adult, even today, I keep a second, spare item in my pantry of any food I really like, to ensure I never run out. My issues of food insecurity run deep. So, I have struggled with my weight going up and down my entire life. I would become overweight and then lose forty to sixty pounds, only to gain it back a couple of years later. I have tried every diet out there. I have been a part of many gyms and physical exercise programs. I have read books on weight loss and participated in support groups.

As I aged and the extra weight led to health issues such as high blood pressure, high cholesterol, diabetes, sleep apnea, and so on, I made the challenging decision to have gastric bypass surgery. With so many of my family members dying young (grandfather at forty-four, older brother at thirty-six, younger brother at forty-two, mother at sixty, husband at fifty-nine), I am too familiar with early deaths. I wanted a different path for myself, and I wanted to ensure my son had at least one parent for as long as possible.

The decision to have the surgery was difficult, however, because I honestly did not want to put my body through another operation. With the issues I had as a child, their consequences that followed into adulthood, and other conditions that have arisen (cancer two times), this weight-loss procedure would be my twenty-fourth surgery. Asking my body to go through an optional procedure seemed almost unfair. Additionally, every time I've been hospitalized, I've had to be prepared for the flashbacks and nightmares that resurface from years ago.

After many hours of talking this through in therapy, I eventually decided the benefits would override the challenges, and I chose to have the surgery. I have made great progress emotionally in my therapy and I began to look at this physical experience as another way of shedding (literally and figuratively) the past and creating the person I want to be, physically and emotionally. As of this writing, it has been over two years since the surgery. I have lost 110 pounds. I no longer take any prescription medications and no longer have high blood pressure, high cholesterol, diabetes, or sleep apnea. Surgery is not the answer for everyone, but for me, it has been one of the best paths I have chosen toward a stronger, healthier me!

While having the surgery has been a tremendously positive

experience, it has not been without its challenges. After countless hours sitting on the bathroom sink as a little girl, staring into the derogatory words written on the mirror in my blood, I have spent a lifetime avoiding mirrors. My father's repeated mantras about my ugliness, and about the distress caused to others who were forced to look at me, trained me to avoid looking at myself. I have walked the earth trying to be as still and as invisible as possible to others and probably, most sadly, to myself.

When, in my career, I became a trainer and found myself standing in front of hundreds or thousands of people and talking for hours, I had to learn to be comfortable with having people look at me. I tried hard to create presentations with material that was interesting and engaging so people would pay more attention to what I was saying than who they were looking at. I used humor to put people at ease and, in my mind, relieve the distress they might be experiencing because of what they had to look at during the presentation.

But when a person loses a great deal of weight, the consequence is that people notice you more. In our society, some people look unfavorably on people who are overweight. Their way of communicating their displeasure is to avoid eye contact. As an overweight person, I was able to stay more invisible because people often avoided looking at me. But when I began losing weight, I discovered more people making eye contact and speaking to me. I could feel my presence being more noticeable, and I had to work through the discomfort of this in my therapy sessions.

Being more noticeable is a relatively new experience for me and an issue that is not completely resolved. Sometimes I think I should have had the surgery years ago, but then I remember, I would not have been emotionally ready to manage the issues that have been stirred up. I had to be different on the inside before I was ready to be different on the outside. I still can't look in the mirror and think, "Good morning, beautiful lady," but neither do I find myself staring at the sink basin while brushing my teeth, just to avoid seeing what is in the mirror. I no longer worry that I am making people physically ill when they look at me and, as always, I enjoy making eye contact and smiling when I meet new people. And now they often smile back.

They say beauty is in the eye of the beholder, and my definition of my own beauty continues to evolve every day. My body has survived many broken bones, hundreds of stitches, two dozen surgeries and countless tortures. I am beginning to wear my physical being with a sense of gratitude and appreciation for all it has been through and survived. I am grateful to have been left with a body that can swim in the lake and hike in the woods and has a lap to hold my dogs, arms to hug my son, eyes that see the beauty in the world, ears to hear laughter, and a heart that beats stronger than ever, allowing me to love the people and the world around me. I am indeed a fortunate woman!

CHAPTER 28

Fear and Terror

*"Nothing in life is to be feared, it is only to be understood.
Now is the time to understand more, so that we may fear less."*
—Marie Curie

MOST OF MY childhood was spent in a continuous state of fear and anxiety. It is not surprising that, years later, when I went to my first appointment with Ed, I never indicated I was seeking happiness but rather that I was in search of peace. Being in a state of fear or anxiousness was so frequent that I had to learn how to recognize those feelings as something other than normal. As with many of my feelings, fear was happening on the inside while I was smiling and functioning on the outside. It was only in my therapy sessions that I began to allow those feelings to come to the surface.

Fear is an absolutely terrifying emotion! I recognize the absurdity of that statement, but it is true. For me, fear is often debilitating as there was only one option in the familiar "fight, flight, or freeze" response, and that was to freeze. Fight, flight, or freeze is a description of our responses to a threat. To fight is to confront the threat aggressively. Fighting my father was not an option. Flight means you run from the danger. I had nowhere to run. When you freeze, you find yourself unable to move or act against the threat. With fight and flight both unavailable to you, you may find yourself hiding from the danger. Most of the time, my response was to freeze.

In recent years, the "fawn response" has been added as a type of response to a threat. The fawn response is when the person complies with the attacker to save himself. I came to the realization that this was the type of response I had most often as a child. That was what I needed to do to keep my father from escalating further.

When people feel threatened, their bodies immediately respond to the danger. Whether they spring into a fight, flight, freeze, or even fawn response, the underlying goal is to minimize, end, or avoid the danger in the situation and return to a state of calm and control.

Every day of my childhood, something would happen that would be a threat to me, and I found myself either freezing or fawning. As an adult walking through a minefield, this response is familiar to me, as events will trigger an old response. Peeling back the layers to discover what is under the fear has been a difficult and time-consuming process. I could easily identify the fear, but understanding what was under it was far more complicated. This was partly because, when I was in a state of fear and activated the freeze response, it was almost impossible to take any action to explore what might be under the surface.

There are many strategies, such as breathing and meditation, that can assist in moving away from fear enough to be able to take action, but when terror is front and center, trying to access strategies of any sort seems almost futile. Ed became very skilled at taking me toward memories enough to access the feelings but not so deep into them that I was paralyzed with fear. As you can imagine, this was a delicate balancing act. Though this method worked more often than it failed, it still slowed progress immensely. After numerous lessons with my father, I had learned how to not fear pain or punishment.

The innate response that remained with me throughout my childhood was a fear of dying. I had a constant sense that my very existence was threatened, and saying or doing the wrong thing would put my life in jeopardy. Heightened by the knowledge that my father really did not want me to be alive, my fear of death felt like a constant companion. It again took many years for me to understand and realize that my father had the full power and means to take my life, but he chose not to because keeping me alive under the threat of death was far more fulfilling to him than actually having me die. So, he always came back to take me out of the cold cellar shortly before I was at risk of starving to death. He always provided me with just enough water for survival. He brought me out and warmed me up just enough to keep me from freezing to death. His cuts were deep enough to cause me to bleed but not so deep as to be life threatening. His beatings would leave bruises, but the bruises were not substantial enough to kill me. If only that little girl could have known his plan, the fear of death might not have had to be a constant companion to every breath I took.

Our garage (or barn, as we called it) was a two-story building that was detached from our house. I don't remember that we ever put a vehicle in there. It was a place for my father to work on whatever he spent hours working on. It is where he stored his snowmobiles and motorcycles. It held a big table saw and, during the winter, his homemade log splitter. It was the building he used to gut his deer after a hunting trip and an escape room for when he did not want to be near any of the family.

In the middle of the ceiling was a trap door and, when he opened it, he could lower a large pulley from the second floor to the ground, for the purpose of lifting heavy objects up on to the second floor. My father was proud of the contraptions he would make—my bottle holder, the wood splitter, this makeshift "elevator," as he called it.

One of my father's most terrorizing games was to put me on the hook of the pulley and lift me to the roof of the second floor of the garage. He would then open the trap door and lay a large bear trap on the floor under the trap door. (It would not have been all that challenging to find a bear trap in Maine.) I am not certain how it worked, but he put the rope of the pulley into another homemade contraption that would release the pulley if there was too much movement on the rope. The objective was for me to hang on the pulley from about twenty feet in the air and remain as still as possible, knowing that too much movement would cause the rope to release, dropping me through the trap door onto the waiting bear trap.

To introduce this lesson to me, he demonstrated the pulley and bear trap action first on a rabbit and then on a neighborhood cat. As I watched both animals be swallowed and killed by the bear trap because they were wriggling so much when placed on the hook, I knew my life was in certain danger if I could not remain very still on this pulley. As much as I tried to prepare myself, the moment he hung me from the hook my body went into a total state of terror as I swung over the trap door, knowing the bear trap was armed and ready to catch me. My father then left, saying he was going out of town for a couple of days. I honestly do not know how long he was gone. It might have been only a day; it might have been several days. I remember being so intently focused on not moving my body that I was terrified when I could not hold back and had to relieve myself, uncertain whether that motion would be enough to drop me to the trap. I remember trying so hard to stay awake, for fear that I would move in my sleep and the rope would release. Some of my father's rituals were done in a manipulative way to induce a fear of dying when he knew all along that he wouldn't actually kill me. Remembering this experience has been terrifying for the reality that his "trap" in this situation could most certainly have resulted in my death.

The reality of this terror surfaced many years later when my therapist would mention that he was "going out of town for a couple of days," even though it had been more than forty years since my father had activated the pulley and bear trap. Fear stays with you. It makes its home in every cell in the body and crouches there, waiting until, years later, a few simple words bring it out of hiding. It has been a deliberate, difficult, and conscious choice to not allow fear to run my life. In the beginning, I thought forgetting everything that had happened to me was the way to peace, but I came to understand that while I may not have been thinking about the memories, they were still living in my cells, in my bones, and in my reflexes. So, I made a choice not to run from my fears but to meet them head on. I do not always win these battles, but I win far more of them now than I did years ago.

> *"FEAR has two meanings: Forget Everything And Run or Face Everything And Rise. The Choice is Yours."*
>
> —Zig Ziglar

I choose to rise.

CHAPTER 29

Peace, Hope, and Love

I HAD MANY feelings buried deep inside that were recovered only through countless hours of difficult therapy work, and most of those were feelings my father had perceived as negative. I have written about several of them (anger, guilt, shame, fear, terror, sadness, grief, and so on) and my struggles to reclaim them in a healthy manner in my life.

I also experience many positive feelings. These include peace, hope, and love. As a measure of my father's failure to win his challenge to change me, I often use my ability to continue to experience love and joy; peace and hope. While I have had to work to understand and feel them to their fullest degree, I have had access to these positive feelings in my relationships with my husband, son, other family, friends, and colleagues.

Peace

"Peace is a daily, a weekly, a monthly process, gradually changing opinions, slowly eroding old barriers, quietly building new structures."

—John F. Kennedy

As mentioned before, the greatest feeling I have been seeking in my therapy is one of peace. I have been searching for a calmness in this world. Originally, I believed finding this sense of peace was about stopping the nightmares and flashbacks. I thought peace would be here when I no longer stepped on land mines and found myself triggered by everyday events. Peace was all about not being afraid anymore. But then I noticed that I slowly began accepting what had happened and how I'd responded to what had happened. I began deciding for myself who I believe I am as a person and not relying on my father's messages. I began to be able to look in the mirror and feel OK with what I saw. I learned to start seeing myself accurately, with my strengths and my weaknesses. I noticed I now have access to all of my feelings and my choices about what to do with those feelings.

The peace I have been seeking from resolving issues is not about past memories or present-day events. It is about experiencing myself with the same love and kindness I express to other people—learning to be as forgiving of *my* shortcomings as I am of those of my col- leagues, friends, and family. What I have discovered is that I don't need to be fixed or created, the way my father tried to do. I have all of the tools I need to be successful in this world. I am compassion- ate and treat people with kindness and understanding. I believe in the goodness of people and hold onto that belief until they give me reason to believe otherwise. What I now understand is that peace will come as I learn to treat myself with the same degree of humanness that I extend to others.

It is almost too cliché to say, but the entire journey toward peace is one of learning to love myself. Every step I take in that direction brings the calmness and peace I have been so desperately seeking. As I look back on this road, I find the journey challenging to describe, but it has been so worth it as I notice the seeds of liking myself grow- ing and even recognize the possibility of loving who I am and what I bring to this world. As I let go of the old ideas of believing I am a mistake who brings only pain and trouble to this world, and see the grace and beauty of what I actually do offer, the peace begins to roll in as one might experience the slowly changing tides of the ocean.

Hope

"When our days become dreary with low-hovering clouds of despair, and when our nights become darker than a thousand midnights, let us remember that there is a creative force in this universe, working to pull down the gigantic mountains of evil, a power that is able to make a way out of no way and transform dark yesterdays into bright tomorrows."

—Martin Luther King, Jr.

More than with most emotions, when writing about hope, I feel most compelled to find the right words. For anyone who has experienced serious trauma in their life, hope is an essential step on the path of recovery, and yet there are moments when it is buried so deep it is unrecognizable. I am fortunate because, once my son was born, no matter how difficult this path became, I knew that suicide was not an option for me because of the damage it would do to him. Having spent a lifetime in therapy trying to heal from the effects of childhood experiences, I have always been determined to ensure that my son did not suffer the consequences of my issues.

Of course, I know this is impossible to accomplish all the time, and he will no doubt experience struggles resulting from my behaviors and messages, but I had to be sure it wasn't to the degree that I had experienced. The impact of my dying by suicide would likely have put him into years of therapy, and it just was not an option. Some would say that clearly delineating that decision made my path easier. I would argue that while it kept me alive, there were moments when that conviction made me feel even more trapped and hopeless. I'm thankful for it, for sure, but it did not necessarily make things easier. Perhaps what it did do was force me to survive at the times I was most hopeless. And there were many of those times.

It is not possible to go back and recover deeply buried emotions that are attached to horrible experiences without facing the extreme trauma that caused those issues. I had to feel as lost, terrified, confused, sad, hopeless, angry, and guilty as a five-year-old girl locked in a cold cellar would feel. What I began to know is that Cheri had many moments where, as much as she struggled to stay alive, she also wished death would just come and take her. It was in these moments that my human instinct for survival was the only thing that carried me through.

Sometimes, hope is not something you can see or hold onto but only something you can count on as a functioning resilience resting silently inside you, in the same way we become unaware of our breathing. Over time, I recognized that even when I'd been at my lowest points, the presence of hope had operated like the blood circulating through my body, without my awareness.

As I began to understand this, I stopped saying that I felt "hopeless" and instead began to trust the process and know that I would eventually begin to feel better and stronger. In the meantime, hope would keep me waking up every day; coming back for my next session; and functioning in my life, just as my body systems kept working, whether I was aware of them or not.

As a child, every day, I hoped I would do whatever I needed to do well enough to survive until the next day. During my years of therapy, I returned several times to a place where the only thing I was hoping for was to make it through another day. And I did. And then I made it through another one after that. And eventually, I began to hope for more than survival. I began to hope for living—fully present living. I began to hope for peace. I began to hope for an opportunity for my words to help someone else.

I noticed a shift from hoping to survive my childhood to finding a way to use it to help others. I think that's what hope does. It helps us look outward to possibilities. It allows us to survive what is happening and holds onto the idea that we can move through to something better—something bigger than ourselves. I chose the field of education because I have always wanted to help others, but in my situation, hope allowed me to see my childhood as a new opportunity to bring light into someone else's darkness. This book is hope coming to life.

Love

"One word frees us of all the weight and pain in life. That word is love!"

—Sophocles

I have had the wonderful opportunity to feel deep love in my life. In the summer between my junior and senior year of college, a friend invited me to her Fourth of July lobster feast because she had another friend she wanted me to meet. I was not a fan of blind dates, so I worked it out with another friend to call me at two o'clock, giving me an excuse to leave the cookout after two hours if the "match" was a disaster. When my friend called at two, I told her I wanted to stay, and Al and I proceeded to have our first date, which lasted fourteen hours. We ate lobster. He took me to Castine to take out his small sailboat. We watched fireworks. We danced in a bar and finally, at 2:00 a.m., we said good night. We made a promise to meet again.

A few days later, I drove to my college town of Orono. Al was a student there as well, but we were both out for the summer. I thought I might take the initiative and see if he wanted to meet for lunch. Unfortunately, I didn't have his phone number with me. Long before the days of cell phones, this meant I needed to pull into a gas station and look up his number in the phone book, so I did exactly that. However, his number wasn't listed. I called information and they didn't have a listing for Al Fuller either. I was beginning to wonder if Al really existed. As I stood at the pay phone trying to remember my friend's phone number, I looked up and Al was at the gas pump, filling his tank. The odds of him being there at that moment were so small, I wonder if it was in that moment that I fell in love, as it seemed fate wanted this to happen.

We were married two years later and moved to Florida. I loved the opportunity to leave behind so much pain from my childhood and begin a new life with this patient, kind, safe, and wonderful man. In the early years of our marriage, my husband and I experienced three miscarriages—one at nine weeks, one at twelve weeks, and one at fourteen weeks. During the fourth pregnancy, at sixteen weeks, I was diagnosed with cervical cancer. The doctor recommended terminating the pregnancy so we could treat the cancer. My husband and I said no.

At twenty-two weeks, during a regular check-up, they repeated the ultrasound three times and required extra bloodwork, and we knew something was wrong. The doctor then told us he thought there was a problem with the baby. He believed the baby would be born with several issues—only one kidney, significant digestive problems from a deformed stomach, and possibly a damaged or missing liver. Again, he recommended terminating the pregnancy. We again said no. We had fought hard for this pregnancy and we were going to see it through no matter what.

At six months, while I was shopping at Home Depot to replace a broken hot water heater, my water broke. Al took me to the emergency room, and they admitted me to the hospital. I had a tear in the top of my uterus. If I lay flat on my back and stayed relatively still (a skill I was well trained for) the fluid my son needed to continue to grow would replenish and he could remain in my belly for a while longer. So, I did. I stayed flat on my back for thirty-one days.

At seven months, our son was born, at just under four pounds. They took him away to the neonatal intensive care unit and it was several hours before I was able to see him. After scrubbing my hands and arms and putting on protective clothing, I went into the unit to meet my son. As I looked down at him, I watched as his tiny chest caved in with every breath, allowing me to see all of his bones. For a moment, I thought I would pass out, but as I moved my eyes to his face, the love I felt in my heart confirmed that, in spite of my father's senseless, horrific, and unrelenting efforts, he hadn't come close to destroying the love my heart is capable of feeling.

From my father's perspective, my sensitive heart was my greatest nemesis; from my perspective, it was my greatest strength. My love for my son and my continued love of children and babies, puppies and kittens, and the goodness of all people are evidence that he was not able to change the essence of my heart. I have learned to embrace my loving and sensitive nature instead of being ashamed of it. It has brought the greatest moments of joy to my life and served as a source of strength when the world felt the darkest.

My now twenty-nine-year-old son is happy and healthy and has been the source of many of those great moments of love and joy. He was born with all of his internal organs completely normal. He has a mild case of cerebral palsy, but it has not interfered in his life in any significant way. Additionally, because he was born early, my cancer was successfully treated two months earlier than planned. From my perspective, love wins every time!

CHAPTER 30

Jealousy and Envy

Jealousy is simply and clearly the fear that you do not have value. Jealousy scans for evidence to prove the point that others will be preferred and rewarded more than you. There is only one alternative—self-value. If you cannot love yourself, you will not believe that you are loved. You will always think it's a mistake or luck. Take your eyes off others and turn the scanner within. Find the seeds of your jealousy; clear the old voices and experiences. Put all the energy into building your personal and emotional security. Then you will be the one others envy, and you can remember the pain and reach out to them.

—Jennifer James

THE DICTIONARY DEFINES *jealousy* as the emotion that occurs when you fear that someone may take something you have. *Envy* is more about the emotion you feel when you want or covet what someone else already has. There are many similarities between these emotions, and I tend to use them interchangeably.

My father worked hard to make sure I was jealous of virtually every other person in my life. He perpetuated the myth that I was "less than" all other people. He used to take me to the grocery store, but instead of getting food, we would "shop" for all the little girls that he would be proud to have as his daughter—and there were lots of them. In fact, I recall only one girl that he said he would not want, because she was too fat and "at least I didn't have that problem." But all the other little girls, from his perspective, were prettier, smarter, stronger, funnier, more helpful, kinder, and overall better candidates to be his daughter. I was so jealous. I believed that if I could just be more like everyone else—anyone else—my father would finally love me, and all of the horrible things happening to me would stop.

I was jealous of my brothers. My father was not a good father to any of us, but he was slightly easier on my brothers because he was proud to have boys. I was envious of how he wanted to teach them things. I was envious of how he talked about them with a sense of pride to his friends. I spent a great deal of my childhood looking at others' lives and being envious, but like with all other emotions, my father punished any hint of jealousy or envy. Once again, he would create situations to evoke the emotion (like picking out better girls at the grocery store) and then conduct painful lessons designed to extinguish the emotion.

Many years later in my therapy, these feelings would begin to surface as I noticed other patients come or go from my therapist's office. Early on in the therapy, there were rare moments I would learn a piece of information about Ed's daughters, and the buried feelings of envy would begin to burn. It took a long time to even admit I was experiencing these feelings and longer still to begin to accept them as a part of myself. I slowly began to understand that what I was experiencing was not about any particular item, event, or relationship, but about the deeply embedded feelings of being unworthy of any of those things I was seeking. As long as I felt undeserving of a loving relationship, I was destined to continue to crave the loving relationships I observed around me. Jealousy and envy were merely symptoms of a much bigger battle I was fighting to develop and grow a positive sense of myself. Part of my measure of growth over time became the shift in the amount of time and attention I gave to thinking about the other people in my therapist's life (his wife, daughters, clients, friends, neighbors). As I grew more confident in my feelings about myself, and as the security of our relationship grew, I began to worry less about how important other people were to him.

I am likely to never reach a complete sense of comfort with the emotion of jealousy or envy, but now I can at least see it as a sign that I need to pay attention to how I am feeling about myself. If I find myself thinking or worrying more about the other relationships Ed has, then I know I am feeling more insecure and less good about myself. Fixing that is not always a fast or easy task, but it is far more likely to happen now that I can identify it so much more rapidly.

An example of how these ideas have shifted for me happened in a session where Ed shared with me a video he had created for his granddaughter's birthday. He had a video of a brightly colored unicorn, and he used his own voice to make the unicorn sing her the happy birthday song. It was adorable, and I felt both joy because it was cute and a sense of connection because he was willing to show it to me.

After he sent it to his granddaughter, he got a video back of both of his granddaughters intently watching it on their parents' phone, mimicking the unicorn and singing along with the video. The two little girls, ages three and five, with blond curls and smiling faces, stirred more feelings in me. I do not have many pictures of me as a child. My father used to use my school pictures for target practice. Most pictures of me he destroyed, as he could not tolerate concrete evidence of such an ugly daughter staring back at him from a photograph. I do have one picture of me sitting on my grandmother's porch at about eighteen months old. My blond curls in that picture reminded me of Ed's granddaughters, and I imagined myself as a cute little girl before I learned to think of myself as ugly. When I saw the video of his granddaughters and thought how adorable they were, I wondered how awesome it would be to think that Cheri was equally as adorable. So, this video stirred many positive feelings for me.

That night, I had horrible nightmares and, even though the next day was Saturday, Ed was willing to do a Skype session with me to process what was going on. As we talked through the event and my evening following it, I told him that, unlike in the past when the video would have stirred strong feelings of envy, I noticed as I was walking to my car a sense of sadness. I didn't wish he was my father or grandfather but instead thought, *I deserved to have someone in my life who would have sent me cute messages on my birthday.*

This boost in self-confidence and shift in feeling worthy of certain positive responses by others resulted in my subconscious giving me a night of punishment. It was a miserable night because my nightmares always have elements that are similar to my reality as a child. So, it's impossible to dismiss them as an event that could not happen or was unlikely to happen. Ed commented on how deeply seeded these old messages are and what a hard-fought battle we are in to change them. It's as though my father lives in me and continues to fight for control. But Ed reminded me that ten years ago the thought "I deserved to have . . ." would never even have come into my mind, and the fact that it did was a cause for celebration and a renewed energy toward fighting the battle.

At the end of the session, I asked Ed if he would consider sending me the two videos so I could watch them again and again, because I am determined to win not only this battle but the war. I will feel good about myself and will use that good feeling to the best of my ability to help others discover that they too can feel good about themselves, even if someone has worked hard to convince them otherwise.

CHAPTER 31

Attachment

"...An incredibly valuable avenue for developing a secure attachment is through therapy. A good therapy relationship allows a person to form a secure attachment with the therapist. Having a corrective emotional experience with someone who can consistently provide a secure base and allows us to feel and make sense of our story is a gift that can benefit us in every area of our lives."

—Lisa Firestone, "Healing from Attachment Issues,"
Psychology Today

THE CONCEPT OF attachment is so huge it could be the subject of an entire book itself. Ultimately, all of my work has been about repairing the damage done from the unhealthy attachments of my childhood. From the moment of birth (and technically before), we are completely dependent upon our parents to care for us in every possible way. When that relationship is insecure, unavailable, or dangerous, the effects are long-lasting and can only be repaired through a tremendous amount of attention and work. I am here to testify—the struggle is *real*!

In my case, my father created an even greater sense of dependence by locking me in the cold cellar and controlling every aspect of my life. I needed him in ways that went beyond the important and normal aspects of parenting—love, affection, security, and so on. I needed him in order to stay alive, and he reminded me regularly that he held that power. All children are dependent on their parents to keep them alive, but it isn't normally communicated as a negotiating strategy for expected behaviors.

When a parent is absent, distant, or abusive it is not an option to walk away or not care. We know we need them, so we are constantly working to keep the attachment present and safe in our lives, in whatever way we need to make that happen. For me, it was about learning my lessons, being available for sex, being as invisible as possible, and meeting any need my father had, as quickly and efficiently as possible. Because keeping him happy was essential to my staying alive, my attachment was perilous and insecure.

As an adult, I recognized my pattern of trying to redo this attachment and come out with a better ending. As I started to get in touch with my needs, I discovered the impossible dilemma of needing to move toward my attachment to establish a feeling of security and reassurance, while simultaneously moving away from the attachment for fear that if the needs were noticed the source of attachment would potentially go away.

This "push/pull" dynamic played out for years between Ed and me. We made tremendous progress on the attachment in the first ten years, as I began to trust how reliable and available he was to me. Developing a sense of security in the attachment then left me free to work through and resolve many of the memories and issues that had created the attachment problems in my early years. Of course, as these surfaced, so did the threat to the present-day attachment, which slowed the progress even further.

The old saying about two steps forward and one step back comes to mind, except the early years felt more like one baby step forward and several giant steps back. Part of the problem was that, as I became aware of the attachment, I openly fought it. I did not want to be attached to this man—to any man. I knew I wanted to feel better, but I needed to remain independent and unattached. I tried endlessly to manage, monitor, and control my level of attachment, only to discover that while I thought I was busy doing that, I really was becoming more attached through every interaction. The attachment ultimately was the necessary piece to my healing, but it also was my greatest adversary. As the attachment began to feel secure, it created space for the memories of my horrific experiences to come out.

And come out they did! Most of the memories were there all along; it was the emotions attached to the experiences that I had not yet explored. When we began to shine light on all of those feelings, I became a totally different person emotionally, and it was not pleasant for me to see myself that way. There were times when I reached out to Ed on a daily basis, and some days, I called multiple times. Our sessions were sometimes as frequent as six days a week. Often, we had to make the sessions longer, going from the regular fifty minutes to seventy-five minutes.

For someone who is not to supposed to show any needs, my neediness came front and center for a period of time, and it was painful to allow that to happen. It took a long time, and it was a big struggle, but eventually we both could see progress. I could manage longer periods of time between communications with him. If I became emotional, I learned to be able to tolerate those feelings without needing to immediately run to Ed for support. If I had a bad night of nightmares and did not have a session scheduled the next day, I could hold a space for that experience and wait to process it at my next session. It was slow, painful, and incredibly expensive, but I had no choice. This process was as necessary to my healing as my heart was to pumping blood through my body.

While the attachment became solid and secure during our normal routine, allowing me to process and grow from so many injuries and issues, the one area that remained a challenge for both of us was when we had a separation due to a vacation or holiday break. It may appear obvious why that would be an issue in those years where I required such frequent contact, but the puzzle was why it continued to be an issue even after so many other problems had reached a greater sense of resolution. For example, when I reduced my therapy to three times per week, we could potentially go from Thursday morning to Monday morning and I would not have difficulty with that time of separation. However, if Ed were going to be going out of town for the weekend, even though we weren't scheduled to meet, I became extremely anxious and reverted to many earlier insecure feelings and behaviors. I could make a pretty extensive list of the many strategies we tried for these separations, including phone calls, using other therapists, texting, Skyping, sending me postcards, sending me pictures, and so on, but it still continued to be a problem.

Part of the dilemma was in my reluctance to make use of some of the strategies he was willing to try. For me, he deserved a vacation (translated—a break from needing to deal with me), so I did not want to call him or make him reach out to me. I believed that if he did not get a break from me, he would become tired of me, and thus my regular attachment when he was in town would be in jeopardy. Additionally, my father used to come back from separations expressing how wonderful it was not to have had to see my face or hear my voice and showing me great distress that he now had to put up with me again. It was painful to experience myself as causing someone that much grief and, as much as I cared about Ed, I could not tolerate seeing or hearing him feel that way about me, so I had to protect the relationship by giving him breaks from me.

The difficulty arose because his going out of town reminded me so much of being abandoned in the cold cellar. This seemed to get resurrected in its worst form whenever he left town. We tried to work on the cold cellar issues, but the greatest feelings did not surface until it was time for him to leave. That meant I was alone with my greatest feelings of need to reach out to him because I was reliving the cold cellar while simultaneously believing that I needed to stay away from him and give him a break so he would be sure to come back. Throw into the mix that I also had to balance this with the fear that he would like the break from me so much he would not want to see me when he returned. It became a pattern that I would cancel my appointments sometimes for two and three weeks after a separation.

The safe and secure attachment that worked so well during our regular schedule seemed to almost disappear the moment he mentioned he would be going out of town. I had some of the same reactions if I were the person going out of town, but not nearly to the degree that occurred when he would go away.

I wish I could describe the magic strategy we finally discovered to ease this issue and make separations easier for both of us, but unfortunately it is one piece that has not completely fallen into place yet. We are making progress, and we've had a few separations that have worked much better than those in the past. In fact, if I can get out of my own way, there is hope that this issue too will be resolved. The solution we are working with right now is to let go of my fears of contacting him when he is away and respond in the same way I did in the early years of therapy—if I needed him, I would reach out to him. We have had a couple of weekends where I was able to do this, and it made a huge difference to the quality of my weekend and my level of anxiety.

After those successful weekends, I also was able to immediately pick up with our sessions when he returned, without canceling. In between those successful weekends, I had a couple of difficult experiences because I convinced myself that I had mastered the issue and would be fine not reaching out, even though I really did need to contact him. I remind myself that when we used the strategy in our regular therapy for me to make contact whenever I needed, I did eventually not need to reach out as often. In fact, now, I go many weeks without reaching out between scheduled sessions, even if our schedules mean we are meeting less frequently. Looking at that pattern, there is reason to believe that just allowing myself (and little Cheri) to reach out when she needs to when he goes away should result in similar successful separations.

I still struggle with the guilt of interrupting him. Our plan includes a reassurance from him that he will tell me if it is not a good time, and when he has done that, I have managed it without difficulty. I have high hopes that I will eventually be able to not need him during vacations and not have such strong emotions when he tells me he is leaving, but as of right now this might be the place where I need to say: to be continued.

CHAPTER 32

Cutting

"Turn Your Pain into Wisdom"
—Oprah Winfrey

I HAVE HAD to learn to be gentle with myself in a way that was never modeled for me during my childhood. I can have a very harsh response to mistakes, issues, or any ideas that would make me appear less than perfect. It is an odd psychological experience to believe so poorly of myself and yet expect perfection in every way. The implication is that if I'm that close to perfect, I must be pretty great, but I never felt great—I felt the opposite. The perfection I was seeking was the harsh conscience I developed as a reflection of my father's expectations of me. Some would say this need to seek perfection is an attempt to control a situation that is totally out of control.

A common strategy I have learned to measure whether I am being too harsh with myself is to think about how I would respond to a child, or one of my teachers, or a neighbor if they behaved in the way I was behaving. I don't like to talk in absolutes, but in this situation, the way I would respond to someone else never matched how I was responding to myself. Part of the way that I needed to learn to be gentler and more forgiving with myself was by recognizing the many issues I have carried into my adult life as a result of my childhood experiences. Every time we would stumble onto a way I was being defensive or not reacting in a "normal" or "healthy" manner, I would become angry with myself. Some of my coping strategies, such as dissociating, have been embarrassing and took years for me to talk openly about with Ed. Even writing some of my realities in this book comes with an apprehension about how people I work with or know will think of me differently, as "crazy" or "broken" or "mentally sick," should they read my book.

Ultimately, one source of healing this book brings me is another opportunity to own who I am and what has happened to me and not hide in shame or embarrassment. That means owning all of it—the good, the bad, and the ugly. And there's lots of ugly.

One tactic I learned early in my life that could help me survive was to cause injury to myself by cutting. Cutting is a type of self-harm, particularly among children, that some use to cope with overwhelming distress, for example, anger, guilt, or pain. I started cutting around eleven or twelve years old. It worsened over the years and, when I was sixteen, homeless, and working my summer job at an ice cream parlor, one of the people I was working with did not believe my explanation of getting scratched by the cat. She contacted the priest from our church, who called me to talk about how I was doing. I had not seen him in a long time.

I did not know it, but after he called me to come in for an appointment, he also called my father (as he and my father continued to be good friends). Halfway through our appointment, my father arrived at the rectory. He saw the cuts and drove me to Bangor to be admitted to the hospital as a suicide risk. I spent only one night there, and it was a scary night. Some of the people on the floor with me had very serious mental health issues, and the entire night, I did not dare to sleep. The next morning, I convinced the psychiatrist that I was not suicidal and that I was cutting just to feel better, but it would never be serious enough to really hurt myself. Fortunately, the doctor believed me and, with an agreement that I would see a psychiatrist on a regular basis and begin taking medication for depression, I was released to go.

I saw the psychiatrist a few times. Each visit lasted no longer than five minutes. He would ask me how I was eating and how I was sleeping. Based on my answers, he would adjust my medication or just tell me to come back the following week. On my fourth visit, he suddenly became more interested in my situation and tried to get me to talk about what was going on with me. I just kept repeating that I was fine and that the cutting was a mistake and I wasn't doing it anymore. He started to tell me that I could share anything with him. He asked me if my problems had to do with sex and informed me that there wasn't anything I could tell him that he hadn't already heard. He said he had a client the day before who was worried because he liked to masturbate into people's shoes. He told me that if I had a secret like that, I could share it with him. I said I was fine and he said he would see me next week. I never went back, and nobody ever asked me about it.

I stopped cutting in places that people could see and concentrated on areas covered by my clothes. For the record, I was not suicidal. Cutting simply offered some relief for me. I know how bizarre that sounds, but because I was living with an idea that I had to be punished or to suffer to earn my life and stay here on earth, cutting was a clever way to buy me time. When I got married and moved out of Maine, I stopped the cutting. It resurfaced later in my therapy, and my need to hurt myself became a primary focus of our work. It continued until I could understand the drive to do harm and learn to feel that I deserved to be alive without needing to sacrifice or feel pain to live.

When we are in pain, we all revert to familiar behaviors, because even if they are harmful, the familiarity brings comfort. Ed never told me not to cut. He told me to call him before I cut, and we would see if we could find another path to relief. Many, many times this worked. A few times it did not, and I cut anyway, and we would go back to analyzing the feelings. He never made me feel crazy or humiliated me because I needed this odd behavior to feel better. What he did do was to share with me that the primary reason he didn't want me to hurt myself was because he cared about me and it made him feel sad for me to experience any more pain in my life. Wow! This was a new and powerful concept for me and, most times I felt like cutting, that knowledge helped me choose a better path.

I have had to learn to respect the strategies my mind and body resorted to in order to survive. The idea that I could have the experience of my childhood and come out of it without any defenses, unhealthy strategies, or issues to be resolved is absurd, and now I spend my time feeling grateful for every way that my mind and body responded that allowed me to be here today.

I'm also very aware of the numerous paths my life could have taken—drug or alcohol addiction, prostitution, domestic violence, homelessness, violent behavior, repeating the abuse on others, and many other common reactions to abuse. I feel so incredibly grateful that my life did not go in those directions, and when I think about the possibilities, I become even more forgiving of the ways the abuse continues to manifest in my life.

CHAPTER 33

Let's Have Some Fun!

"There's no fear when you're having fun!"
—Will Thomas

GIVEN THE SADNESS and pain I experienced throughout my childhood, one would think I would be ready and anxious to have some fun. I suppose on some level, I'm more than ready. But when I was a child, fun was not only absent but dangerous. My father would drive by the playground at school to make sure I was not outside playing and having fun. I was not permitted to have friends. I was limited in my interactions with my family. I was exposed to fun, but it was always as a spectator. The message communicated was that fun was for the people who deserved it and, until I was fixed, I did not deserve it. If my father caught me looking longingly at my brothers in the yard having fun, I was immediately banished to the cold cellar. A kitten who got caught playing with my shoelace after I fell asleep in my spot on the den floor was later used as a lesson for me about not having fun as I was forced to strangle the kitten with the shoelace.

So now that I am an adult, fun does not come naturally to me. People who know me would be surprised to hear that, because I often use my sense of humor to create feelings of joy and laughter with others. And I do have fun with that, but it often has been about conscious efforts to create something positive in the presence of others, so they don't regret being with me. With that thinking, it is no longer fun but a penance to be served.

In the privacy of my own life, I am as tentative with fun as I am with many other ideas that require giving up control. So, now I'm learning to have fun and, while it seems it should be easy, it actually is quite difficult. We have learned that every step I take toward reclaiming my natural tendencies (and I do think I am a person that naturally likes to have fun) comes with its reactions, flashbacks, nightmares, and many hours of analysis. I refuse to give up, however. Again, it feels like a battle to win back my life, and I am in it to win it! I recently took a glassblowing class. I bought a jet ski to ride on my lake. And my niece has me almost convinced to sign up for dancing lessons.

I have some long-held beliefs about my abilities (or inabilities) that it is important for me to challenge. Having spent a lifetime being as quiet as possible, I have begun to sing in my car, and the other day, of course in the privacy of my own home, I was singing and dancing to American Pie, which happens to be a very long song, allowing me several minutes of breaking out of my shell. That night in my night-mares, I dreamt that I was so selfishly caught up in having my own fun that I failed to notice that I was dancing on top of a litter of puppies, and inevitably, I stepped on them until their heads exploded and they all died. I woke up in a cold sweat and had to stay awake for several hours to shake off the intense guilt the dream had created. But it was worth it.

I am going to continue looking for every possible avenue to have fun. I have discovered that I love to travel. I believe there is a part of me that remembers feeling so confined by that cold cellar that I now relish the freedom to go anywhere I want and see as many beautiful sights as possible. I am grateful for my therapy, which allowed me to process my first experiences with genuinely having fun, because in the beginning they weren't fun. I have noticed though that the mo-ments of fun and joy now create fewer moments of pain and stress.

It has been a challenge to let go of an image of myself as a person who is meant to suffer. Instead, I embrace the opportunity to engage in experiences that make me feel good. I have spent a great deal of my life living with fear. I have noticed that when I am immersed in fun, there is no fear. The fear may be present as I anticipate the fun and it may show up again afterward, when I think about what I have done, but when I am actually experiencing the fun, there is no room for fear. It feels so freeing to live in those moments when fear is not at all present. I am going to continue to seek out every one of those moments. Watch out world—I'm coming for you!

CHAPTER 34

My Covenant

IN RECENT YEARS, as I have struggled to understand who I am and who I want to be, separate from my father's (and other's) interpretation of me, I found it helpful to write out a covenant to guide my thoughts and behaviors. This covenant is always a work in progress as I continuously examine who I am and how I wish to be in this world. I encourage others to determine the values and ideas that are important for you as you move to become the person you desire to be throughout your healing process. I share mine with you to solidify my own commitment to my ideal self and to serve as a catalyst for your own thinking remembering that everyone's covenant needs to match entirely who they desire to be.

My Covenant

*When I live my best life, I use all of my actions and words to help others to live their best lives.

*As a parent, I choose to help guide my son in whatever way possible that will lead him to his greatest opportunity for success in the life he chooses. When my son looks to me for support, he will see the deepest level of love, respect and confidence in him that I can possibly reflect back to him.

*In my work, I will use my knowledge and skills to teach and support in every way I am equipped. I will use words that demonstrate kindness, empathy and compassion. My actions will demonstrate patience and tolerance for perspectives that may differ from mine. When involved with others in group tasks, I will work in a cooperative manner and use my leadership skills to guide us forward while recognizing those opportunities where my role is to follow and support others who may be leading. I will hold myself and those I work with to a high degree of moral and ethical integrity to better serve those in our care.

*When I have the opportunity to once again have a partner in my life, I will give to the relationship the experience of honesty, trust, compassion, love and grace. I will be authentic and open with my feelings and needs and be responsive and flexible in meeting my partner's needs. I will choose to listen more than talk, understand more than criticize and move toward an intimate connection rather than isolate and avoid.

*I will live a positive life of gratitude and appreciation for the many gifts bestowed on me and I will use those gifts to help others. I will use my sense of humor to help others experience laughter and to feel comfortable and relaxed in my presence. When I meet with financial success, I will be generous in giving support to those who are burdened with obstacles that keep them from the positive experiences I am privileged to have. When I determine how to use the hours in my days, I will ensure that some of my time is spent volunteering with individuals and organizations who can benefit from my knowledge and experiences. I choose to use the abusive and traumatic experiences of my childhood to make me a more empathic and skilled supporter of others who have experienced trauma and abuse and to assist them in their healing journey.

*My presence in the world will be guided by my loving heart. I choose to be friendly and respectful to every individual I am fortunate to meet. I will use my skills of empathy and compassion to value those who come to me with a different perspective or understanding of the world. When someone who is not behaving as their best self, hurts or injures me in some way, I will respond with grace and understanding recognizing connections to others can sometimes be challenging and painful. However, if I find myself with another person or people who do not allow me the opportunity to be my authentic self or in some way continue to bring me harm, I will remove myself from the situation or relationship and instead move to sources of energy that support and reinforce who I know myself to be.

*I will honor my sensitivity and attraction to living things by always being a positive caregiver to animals in my life. I will be patient and understanding knowing that animals cannot process and behave at the higher level of the human experience. When I am aware that others are not treating animals as they should be, I will use my voice and available resources to step in and correct the situation. I will offer love and affection to my fur babies multiple times a day for every day I am honored to have them in my life.

*In relationship with myself, I honor my past by striving to continue to understand all of my feelings, thoughts, needs and behaviors and use this knowledge to develop a healthy and positive sense of myself. I will honor the fortitude and resilience of my physical body in surviving numerous violations by making healthy choices in food, exercise and lifestyle. I respect the damage done to my emotional being by choosing to be authentic in my feelings and expressing all of my emotions in an appropriate manner that leads me to a life of healthy, intimate connections with others. When I feel afraid, sad, guilty, angry or lonely, I will work to understand those feelings and use my understanding of myself and my available resources to move through my feelings and forward into the feelings of security, peace, joy and connection that I understand I am capable of experiencing in my life. When I make mistakes, I will offer myself the same opportunity for grace and forgiveness that I am able to give to others. I choose to treat myself with the same degree of compassion, acceptance, kindness and love that I am more easily able to give to others. I will then take this love out into the world and help others to experience their best lives. I will live my life as recognition of the precious gift it is and offer myself in service to others.

Afterword

"Some people come into our lives and quickly go. Some stay for a while, leave footprints on our heart, and we are never, ever the same."

—Flavia Weedn

I HAVE BEEN writing this book for years. There have been times when writing it felt important and necessary and others when it felt foolish and insignificant. The writing process has been fraught with much the same turmoil and study that my therapy process has evoked.

One of my challenges in writing the book has been to find an ending. I have made tremendous progress and growth over the years in resolving issues, healing old wounds, and discovering peace and joy in life, something that, years ago, I could barely have imagined. But it is not over. I am slowly coming to the realization and acceptance that the journey of recovering from my childhood will never come to an end.

I used to think that was because I was doing something wrong—I wasn't trying hard enough or learning enough information. I wasn't practicing the right strategies or reading the right books. But now, I don't see the ongoing challenges as a failure. I see them instead as a reflection of the depth of the damage that was done. It is not surprising that it could potentially take my entire life to overcome all of the harm that occurred, and that's not because I'm not smart enough to get it or not working hard enough. It's because it was a horrible experience that went on for years, at a time when all parts of my brain and body were in their most vulnerable points of development.

But while I might always live with the consequences of my childhood experiences, I know my childhood doesn't have to define my present-day life. It does not have to deprive me of peace and joy. It does not have to rob me of loving and intimate relationships. It does not have to steal from me the opportunity to love and care for myself and others. It does not have to keep me trapped in darkness and fear.

But while my journey to recovery doesn't need to have an ending, a book does. In the foreword of this book, I described a picture of a heart that had been broken into pieces and how strong that heart could be when it was glued back together—perhaps in some ways even stronger than before it was broken. But the lines where it was broken will always show. I believe all the pieces of my heart are back in place, and my work now is about strengthening the weak spots— deciding which areas might need a little more glue and rubbing down some of the seams where the breaks occurred so they aren't quite so visible. It will continue to be a work in progress.

As I complete this book, an important chapter is about to be written. After Ed and I have worked together for almost twenty years, Ed has decided to retire and move to another state. As I write this, just last week, the offer he made on his new home was accepted and a firm timeline is in place. He will be moving in about two months. This information is not new to me. He has given me plenty of notice, and we have been talking about and processing what this means for over a year now.

Although—true confession—if you'd talked to me the day he officially bought his new house, you might have thought from my reaction that he had never mentioned the idea. I'm scared. That might be an understatement—I'm terrified. Ed has indicated he does not want to be a hundred percent retired and really enjoys his work, so he has offered to keep me on as a client, and we would do our sessions via Skype. When I moved to my lake house two years ago, we started doing some of our sessions through Skype so I would not have to drive the seventy-five minutes to and from his house.

Technology is a true gift to me in this situation, but Skype is not exactly the same as the security and familiarity of being in Ed's house. The occasional needed hug will no longer be an option. And the warm feeling of someone's physical presence will be harder to acquire through an Internet connection. I also have the old familiar fears that once he is away from me and discovers how much he enjoys his new life, there will not be a place for me. The 2020 Cheryl wants only the best for him and believes he deserves a wonderful retirement, free from any work commitments. Beyond what he has done with dozens of other clients, I know he has earned it just from the many years of work with me.

But little Cheri does not want to be left behind. She wants to always feel like she is an important part of his life and he is an important part of hers. I guess this is the part where I learn the normal life experience of letting go of someone important to me and embracing the unknown of the future. I am uncertain of how it's going to go, but I am confident that I now have more skills, strategies, strengths, and awareness than I have ever had in my life to deal with the emotions and experiences that this change is sure to bring.

Writing this book has been another step toward letting the light into the darkest parts of my history. The first years of my life were riddled with secrecy and darkness, stillness and repression, quietness and fear, and violence and hatred. The rest of my life will be filled with peace and joy, light and laughter, openness and transparency, and love and kindness. It is sure to still have pain (flash forward to the moving van pulling away from Ed's house), but it will be pain that I can feel and express. Pain that doesn't come from craziness but from natural loss. Pain that is not twisted and mangled with lies and manipulation but is pure and honest, from an important relationship changing or ending.

So, it seems this may be the perfect time to end this book, as it is a time for new beginnings. While it's a bit cliché and melancholy to say so, the storm is over, and it is time to enjoy the sunshine. It is time to share my story with anyone who happens to pick up this book, and hopefully I get to realize my dream of using the horrors of my experience to bring a little light to someone who is sitting in the dark, holding onto their own pain and suffering through their own nightmares.

I have lived in the darkness. I have stared at evil in its most human form. I have felt pain screaming from every cell in my body. And I have felt despair deeper than the depths of hell. But through it all, no matter what was done to me, I held on to the one thing that would triumph over evil, bring light to the darkest corner, ease my pain and misery, and lift me from the depths of hell. I held on tightly to my capacity to love. My heart, while it often felt stomped on and broken, never stopped being able to love. This journey has been about learning to give some of that love to myself, and it has been the hardest of all the battles I have had to fight.

The reward, however, is getting back my life. Over time, the terror, the grief, the guilt, and the anger have begun to subside and, slowly but surely, the peace I have been seeking has found its way into my life.

For anyone reading this book, I wish you the courage to keep fighting your battles so that you might find that love is the path that will lead you to the peace you deserve. Having known the darkness, you too will bask in the light!

CPSIA information can be obtained
at www.ICGtesting.com
Printed in the USA
FSHW010632060521